BILINGUAL SELECTIONS FROM SOPHOCLES' *ANTIGONE*

AN INTRODUCTION TO THE TEXT

FOR THE GREEKLESS READER

JOAN V. O'BRIEN

Southern Illinois University Press

CARBONDALE AND EDWARDSVILLE

Feffer & Simons, Inc.

LONDON AND AMSTERDAM

Library of Congress Cataloging in Publication Data
Sophocles.
Bilingual selections from Sophocles' Antigone.

Includes bibliographical references.
I.   O'Brien, Joan V.   II.   Title.
PA4414.A7202   1977   882'.01   76-50116
ISBN 0-8093-0826-6

Grateful acknowledgment is made for permission to
quote from the Oxford Classical Texts edition of
Sophocles' Fabulae, edited by A. C. Pearson, 1924.
Used by permission of the Oxford University Press,
Oxford.

CONTENTS

PREFACE

From the theater of Dionysos in Periclean Athens to the Vivian
Beaumont Theatre at New York's Lincoln Center, audiences have
felt the power and the grandeur of Sophocles' Antigone. Commentators from Byzantium to Australia have tried to analyze the
source of its enduring appeal. Playwrights such as Gide and
Cocteau, Anouilh and Brecht have all adapted the play. Translators of various periods, such as H. D. F. Kitto and Richard
Emil Braun in our own day, have tried to transfer the magic of
the original into their respective vernaculars. The commentators have each caught aspects of the play's greatness without,
however, really accounting for its personal appeal to theater-
goers so far removed from the Attic stage. The various playwrights' adaptations are a collective tribute to the play's
continued vitality, but these works naturally tell us far more
about Anouilh and company than they do about Sophocles. And
the limitations of the finest translations, especially for a
work of dramatic poetry, are self-evident. One needs to hear
the poet's own words, his rhythmic effects, antitheses and
repetitions, in order to experience much that is essential to
his art.

So the play remains its own best spokesman and its language
is ancient Greek. Obviously, in a nonphilological age like our
own, the language barrier is formidable. Few shortcuts in the
steep path to mastery of a language have been found. But there
are ways of fascinating, enticing, and cajoling students into
the combination of sprinting and crawling necessary to scale

heights of Mount Parnassos.

The enticements that this book can offer the reader are
fairly impressive: not only Apollo and the Muses at the moun-
taintop but Sophocles and the Theban royal family as fellow
travelers. And for the moments of anguish en route, Antigone
and Creon can surely provide appropriate laments.

Despite the facetious tone, the point is quite serious. In
effect, the book invites the reader to become a student of
ancient Greek in the company of a great playwright and one of
his finest creations.

For the reader with little or no previous exposure to Greek,
the Bilingual Selections is the tool for the first part of the
journey, and the Guide to Sophocles' "Antigone": A Student
Edition with Commentary, Grammatical Notes, and Vocabulary[1] can
soon provide supplementary help. Only selections from the play
are treated in these books so that the student will graduate
from these crutches to an annotated school text, the standard
grammars, and lexica for the final leg of the journey. It may
well be that few will actually scale the heights of Parnassos
via this route. That remains to be seen. But even from the
limited perspective of these books, the general reader, compar-
atist, or student of drama can feel the direct, simple antithetical style of the poet, his quite modern restraint before the
possibilities of language, his objectivity that becomes a blaz-
ing light on human actions. And concomitant with these insights
will be the delight of discovery and decipherment as the reader
begins to see how the language works.

What, then, is the nature and suggested use of the Bilingual
Selections? The book provides an interlinear text of seven
selections from the Antigone and an accompanying literal translation; there are also summaries of the intervening portions of
the play (comments on the Ode on Atē and the Ode on Eros), an
introductory essay on Antigone as an androgynous heroine, the
Greek alphabet, and a short appendix of grammatical terms. For
two of the selections, the Prologue and the Ode on Man, a transliteration (i.e., the writing of Greek words in equivalent letters of the English alphabet) is also provided. Thus, the
beginner can learn the alphabet as he studies the Prologue, and

a student of literature can study the famed Ode on Man without
necessarily studying the whole book.

The enterprising Greekless reader, then, can use the Bilingual Selections as a way of getting behind the verbiage of the
translator. He can see what Sophocles actually said.[2] And the
bald, prosaic translation that accompanies the text reveals in
a negative way important aspects of the poet's art: the un-
adorned nature of his vehicle; the great importance of balance,
word order, and antithesis in his poetry; the conservative use
of "stretching" in metaphors and theme words; and the impossi-
bility of transferring the art of the original into English
without adornments unnecessary in the Greek.

The choice of passages from the play may appear arbitrary,
since there is no way of doing a satisfactory "selective" reading from a classic of such economy. All the passages are chosen because they readily illustrate the poet's diction and
style and the play's ironic structure. All, too, reveal the
characters of the antagonists, Antigone and Creon: three are
character studies of the heroine, three of King Creon, and the
seventh, the Ode on Man, gives some of the playwright's deep-
est thoughts about what it is to be truly human. The ode is
also included because of its great interest to scholars in many
fields.

The three Antigone passages are the Prologue (1-99), Antigone's ecstatic yet simple Defense of the Unwritten Laws (450-
70), and a portion from her last speech (891-928). The first
two show the principle and passion Antigone needed for the
daring burial of her brother. Her last speech, in sharp contrast to the heroic Defense of the Unwritten Laws, includes an
apparently hysterical claim that her real reason for burying
Polynices was that he was her brother--she would not have done
it for husband or child. The passage has embarrassed and of-
fended most modern commentators. They consider the argument
"silly" and contradictory of Antigone's noble motivation.
Thus, they have sought and found some reasons to expunge the
passage from the text. Therefore, this selection is included
so that the student may, from the text itself, study its authenticity and appropriateness.

The Creon passages include his initial, apparently strong, address to the elders (162-214), his confrontation with his gentle but firm son Haemon (631-765), and the end of the king's lament (1284-1353) over his dead son and dead wife. This last passage completes the unmasking of the pitiable king and, by ironic contrast, helps the audience perceive in retrospect that Antigone is indeed a wonder among men, as the Chorus in the Ode on Man unwittingly described her. The episode with Creon's son is a decisive step in the unmasking, and it also shows how Haemon's character complements that of his absent fiancée.

The brief Grammatical Appendix is modest in scope and aims. It makes no attempt to provide an introduction to Greek syntax or to Sophoclean usage. Rather its very limitations direct the student to the standard grammars.[3] It does, however, serve four modest purposes: it describes some unfamiliar grammatical terms, it provides the personal endings of the most commonly used verb forms, it gives some information about common verb and adjective usage, and it serves as a bridge to the more technical material of the Guide.[4]

While the primary audience of the Guide is the intermediate Greek student, its commentary and grammatical aspects were so designed to provide a transition for the Greekless reader from amateur to student. Thus, I hope the reader of this book will use the Commentary and Grammatical Notes of the Guide alongside the interlinear Sophoclean text provided here. At a glance, he or she can see Sophocles' words, a translation, and commentary or grammatical notes. By studying these two books with a standard grammar, then, Greekless students have the tools for serious penetration of the text.

On the matter of the spelling of Greek proper nouns, consistency is virtually impossible. On the one hand, current practice favors restoration of Greek orthography: e.g., Kolonos, Dionysos, Herodotos, instead of Colonus, Dionysus, Herodotus. On the other hand, it seems advisable to leave familiar names in easily recognizable form: e.g., Sophocles, Creon, Eurydice, Tiresias, instead of Sophokles, Kreon, Eurydike, Teiresias.

I hope that the teacher of classical civilization will find

the <u>Bilingual Selections</u> a helpful tool for teaching one play
in some depth. It has been so used on both undergraduate and
graduate levels. I recently used parts of this text with a
graduate English class in Greek tragedy, a class in which only
a handful knew any Greek. The close contact with Sophocles'
language made it possible for us to achieve a far higher level
of image and theme analysis than is usual. Also, readings by
the Greek students of an episode and of the Ode on Man gave the
others some sense of the normal iambic flow of the dialogue and
of the intricate beauty of the lyric rhythms. If experimental
texts like this become common, perhaps they should include
records by gifted Hellenists.

In the Preface to the <u>Guide</u>, I acknowledged family, colleagues,
and friends without whose help the <u>Guide</u> and this book would
never have been completed. Here I wish to add my undergraduate
assistant, Sandra Moffitt, and our departmental manuscript
typist, Elline Long. I thank Elline for typing the English
portions of this text. And a special thanks must go to Sandra
for designing and typing the interlinear pages of the text.
No one who has not coped with the intricacies and frustrations
of the production Sandra undertook can fully appreciate the
magnitude of the task.

Joan V. O'Brien

Carbondale, Illinois
November 1976

INTRODUCTION

Androgyny in the *Antigone*

Like all great classics, the Antigone has survived a plethora
of commentators and editors whose efforts to analyze the play's
power have met with varied success. There is, of course, no
satisfying, much less "correct," reading of a play that is as
rich with animating tensions as the Antigone. Thus, it is
quite natural that respected critics like Calder, Kitto, and
Müller take diametrically opposite positions on aspects of the
play. I have duly noted these conflicting views in the Commentary of the Guide. Therefore, I feel free here to present my
own quite subjective, perhaps idiosyncratic, view of one
neglected dimension of the play. I wish to argue that the
character of Antigone and, to a lesser degree, that of her
fiancé, Haemon, exhibit what we may call "androgyny," a wholeness that blends traditional "masculine" and "feminine"
strengths.[1] Critics have always noted the persistence of the
man-woman theme in the play and have often observed the reversal of traditional sex roles in the rebellious Antigone and her
conciliatory fiancé. They have noted too that the attractive,
"womanly" Ismene would have been far more acceptable to Sophocles' audience that her "unnatural" sister (see Guide, notes
on lines 18-19, 41-43, 678-80); and that Creon's narrowly
patriarchal view of woman would probably have seemed quite
appropriate to the fifth-century B.C. viewer. But I wish to
suggest here that the playwright created a heroine who manifests a blend of "masculine" and "feminine" traits that perhaps
makes her the first androgynous heroine in classical tragedy.

By concentrating on this one theme, I do not mean to infer that
the play is either a tract on androgyny (Sophocles would not
have thought in these categories) or A Doll's House, ancient
style. Nothing is further from the truth or from my intention.
If one were to look for a champion of woman's rights among the
Attic tragedians, Euripides would better qualify. But the fact
remains that it is Sophocles' creation,[2] Antigone, rather than
Euripides' Phaedra, Medea, Alkestis, or even Aeschylus' Clytemnestra who is, I believe, drama's first androgynous heroine.
And if Carolyn Heilbrun's survey of androgynous figures is
complete, Sophocles' feat was perhaps not equaled until Shaw
created his Saint Joan.[3]

I define androgyny as a wholeness of character resulting
from a melding of traditional "masculine" and "feminine"
strengths. I use quotation marks throughout so as to avoid any
judgment on either sex's predisposition to "masculine" or
"feminine" strengths. These traditional labels, now widely
questioned and often discredited,[4] nevertheless had the validity of an almost universal sanction in the past.

First, then, I shall try to illustrate Antigone's androgyny
both from within the play and from a brief comparison of her
character with that of Ajax, the hero of Sophocles' other
extant play of the same period. Then, I shall briefly examine
Haemon's "gynecandrism," a term coined to suggest the predomi-
nance of the "feminine" dimension in his androgyny. The
resulting picture intimates that the dramatist saw the couple
as a new model for effective human conduct, a model vastly
superior to the narrowly "masculine" Creon or the narrowly
"feminine" Ismene.

ANTIGONE'S ANDROGYNY

Antigone's "masculine" qualities include her daring, her
strength of will, her independence, and a desire for glory; she
notably lacks another "masculine" trait, logical reasoning.
Her "feminine" qualities include a tenderness for those she
loves, a passionate excess in protecting their rights, association with and concern for life's victims, an inductive and

instinctive way of reasoning, and a conviction that the truly
humane acts constitute genuine piety. At the same time, she
lacks the most "feminine" of virtues, obedience. In some of
these traits, she resembles Ajax; in some she is quite different. I shall refer to Ajax only insofar as the comparison
sheds light on Antigone.

Ajax, the greatest Greek defensive hero at Troy, is the subject of Sophocles' other extant play in the 440s B.C., the
golden moment of Periclean Athens. The <u>Ajax</u>, it may be
recalled, is set in the Greek encampment near the end of the
Trojan War, and the action opens with the goddess Athena
explaining to her favorite, Odysseus, how Ajax attempted to
kill his fellow Greek chiefs the previous night and how she
robbed him of his sanity so that he mangled sheep instead of
men. Then Ajax emerges triumphantly from his tent, still
bloodied from the animal gore, but grateful to Athena because
he is deluded into thinking she helped his enterprise. His
exuberance over his accomplishment is matched by a savage
appetite for the task yet ahead: the murder of his archenemy
Odysseus. Ajax assures Athena that this cunning fox helplessly
awaits his fate. Thereupon, the hero disappears inside his
tent to complete his "work" against "Odysseus," in reality
another helpless animal. So the Prologue ends as Athena mocks
and Odysseus pities the duped hero. The following episodes
detail Ajax's return to sanity, his realization of Athena's
complicity in his degradation, his feigned acceptance of submission to the Greek chiefs,[5] his compassion for his wife, but
concomitantly, his decision to regain his noble stature by a
self-serving suicide. He dies, then, a lone survivor of the
world of heroic individualism.

One of the persistent themes of both the <u>Ajax</u> and the <u>An-
tigone</u> is the necessity of yielding to forces beyond one's
control: in the <u>Ajax</u> this yielding most frequently takes the
form of <u>sophrosyne</u>; in the <u>Antigone</u>, <u>peitharchia</u>. The two
virtues, <u>sophrosyne</u>, prudence or safe-mindedness, and
<u>peitharchia</u>, obedience, were considered the "feminine" virtues
par excellence and were inscribed on the tombstones of Athens'
good women. Moreover, most classical writers valued <u>sophrosyne</u>

as a cardinal virtue even for men. But Sophocles saw it as a
characteristic of the weak, whether male or female. Thus, in
his plays, sophrosyne and peitharchia are most evident in
characters such as Antigone's sister Ismene and Ajax's captive
wife Tekmessa who, despite their integrity and attractiveness,
are not strong enough to do anything but submit. Ismene reluc-
tantly concludes that she knows her duty to her dead brother
but will have to obey King Creon's order to leave his body unburied. For "we are ruled by those stronger than we," she
admits (63). Other seemingly stronger personalities like Creon
ultimately learn obedience. The king, who early in the Antigone speaks with such authority and apparent self-confidence,
finally collapses and adopts Ismene's word, peisomai, "I shall
obey" (1099).

Ajax, too, seems at one point (Ajax 666 ff.) to accept both
sophrosyne and peitharchia: "From now on I shall know how to
yield to the gods and shall learn to reverence the sons of
Atreus. They are our rulers and they must be obeyed." Like
the wind's blast, he must slacken and give way (Ajax 669 ff.).
But it soon becomes clear that learning the "wisdom"
(sophronein) of slackening sail before the sons of Atreus is
something Ajax will never do. The poet underlines the contrast
between Ajax here and Creon in the Antigone by the fact that
Creon's son Haemon borrows Ajax's images and argument as he
pleads with his father to slacken sail and to relent in his
condemnation of Antigone (710-18). But unlike Creon, the
intransigent Ajax never bends.

So, too, Antigone. In sharp contrast to her sister's
"womanly" acceptance of their uncle's decree forbidding the
burial of their traitorous brother, Antigone's rebellion from
the legal decree is swift, defiant, and final (69-77, 96-97).[6]

In fact, both Ajax and Antigone not only reject the "feminine" virtues of obedience and "wise" moderation but they display qualities antithetical to sophrosyne and peitharchia.
Both are characterized as deinos, an untranslatable word whose
basic meanings include terrible, strange, excessive, and rigid
(see Guide, note on line 332); both are independent, willfully
following an inner law, deciding and acting in isolation; and

both see their deeds are worthy of heroic glory, kleos. These
are mostly "masculine" attributes, although deinos in some of
its meanings has, as we shall see, "feminine" connotations.

What, then, constitutes Ajax's heroism? It is, I believe,
his ferocious self-assurance that his act of savage killing is
in accord with the Homeric ideal of doing harm to his enemies
(Ajax 839-43) and his willingness to take his own life in order
to remain true to the ideal. As a result of his solitary decision in the pre-Prologue, he murders the sheep whom he mistakes
for his enemies; this savage deed is for him a kompos, a glorious deed that establishes his heroic worth (Ajax 90). The
truly noble, he concludes, must either "nobly live or nobly
die" (Ajax 480-81). Any other course is ignoble (Ajax 473).
Only by suicide will his Homeric glory remain untarnished.
Others advise him to soften, to become a man of sense. The
seer Kalchas sums up Ajax's character and fate from the view-
point of a believer in sophrosyne: "Whenever a mere human
thinks thoughts too high for man, his excessive and conse-
quently useless humanity falls in oppressive disaster sent by
the gods" (Ajax 758-61).

Deinos and ōmos are two words that resonate throughout the
Ajax. Tekmessa aptly characterizes her lover as ho deinos
megas ōmokratēs, "the great terrible man of untamed might"
(Ajax 205). He is deinos in his passionate refusal to accept
the limitations either of his own humanity or those imposed by
society, and in his awesome victory over all opposing forces.
He is ōmos, savage, literally, "raw," in the means by which he
achieves his goals: in his savage attack against his supposed
enemies, in his uncivilized disregard for Tekmessa's cries.
Like the deinos anthrōpos, the wonderfully strong hunter and
subjugator, of the first half of the Ode on Man in the Antigone, he conquers all the forces of nature that stand in his
way; but unlike the Chorus of the second half of that ode, he
sees no flaw inherent in his violence. Indeed, when he prays
that his son will be broken in to "his father's savage ways"
(Ajax 548), it is clear that the savage way of life is, in a
very real sense, his ideal.

Antigone does not resemble Ajax in savagery, even though the

Chorus once calls her ōmos (471-72). However, she is a deinos anthrōpos, a wonderfully strange, terrible human being in the Ajaxian mold. How so?

Like Ajax, she made her decision to defy Creon's edict and to bury her brother in the solitary darkness of the pre-Prologue. Like Ajax, and unlike Ismene, Tekmessa, and Creon, she never asks anyone else ti drasō, "what am I to do," a fact recognized by the Chorus who grudgingly call her "independent" and "self-willed." She makes her dangerous decision known to Ismene in a single hammer blow: keinon d'egō thapsō, "him I shall bury" (71-72). The phrase punctuated by an emphatic full stop at the end of the first foot in the line echoes Agamemnon's similar pronouncement in the Iliad when he refused to release Chryseis (Iliad 1. 29): tēn d'egō ou lusō, "her I shall not release!" But unlike Agamemnon's empty blustering, Antigone's boast is an Ajaxian kompos. Kompos, it will be recalled, can mean an empty boast or "an unabashed assertion of one's own worth."7 "Zeus abhors the kompous of a proud tongue" (127-28), the Chorus insists as it denounces the arrogant traitor, Polynices. And the original audience, fresh from hearing Antigone's boast that she will provide the traitor burial, might be tempted to apply this pejorative use of kompos to her.

But for Antigone, the burial of her brother is the only act open to her, and so although she does not use the word kompos, her act is "an unabashed statement of her heroic worth" as well as an act of love and piety. She is fully aware both of the consequences and of the nobility of her proposed act: kalon moi touto poiousēi thanein, "In so doing, I shall die a noble death" (72). The emphatic words are kalon, "noble," and thanein, "to die." Like Ajax in his proud resolve "nobly to live or nobly to die," she fully understands that her act will bring both glory and death.

But she quickly adds words whose tenderness betrays her most elemental motivation: philē met' autou keisomai, philou meta, "I shall rest with him, faithful to his love." The repetition of the initial love-component, philē...philou, reveals the tenderness of her sisterly love. The Homeric ideal is, of

course, to do good to one's _philoi_ and to harm one's enemies.
Ajax emphasizes the second half of the ideal and she the first:
he maintains personal honor against personal enemies; she maintains personal honor by living out her love for a _philos_, her
brother. Neither hero totally ignores the other half of the
ideal: Ajax loves Tekmessa, and Antigone curses her judges
(925 ff.). Still, these secondary emotions do not influence
their respective acts.

Antigone resembles Ajax, too, in her "masculine" or active
attitude toward grief. Woman is a "most pity-loving creature,"
Ajax insists (_Ajax_ 580). And drama critic Thomas Henn seems to
concur. He suggests that most often "the woman's part" in
tragedy is to be "the supreme evoker of pity; to offset the
heroic mood in man."[8] Pity, in its usual definition, is the
emotion one feels for another's suffering, but the word usually connotes a slight contempt because the other person is
seen as defenseless and, therefore, weak. Odysseus tries to
accord Ajax such pity (_Ajax_ 121-22). By her readiness to die,
Antigone no less than Ajax refuses such pity.

A comparison of two lines, one spoken by Tekmessa (_Ajax_ 810)
and one by Antigone (91), shows the two women's profoundly
different attitude toward their respective tragic circumstances. When faced with the ominous news that something
dreadful will befall her Ajax, Tekmessa lovingly vows to "go
as far as my strength allows." As she asks for advice (_Ajax_
809, 920) and protection (_Ajax_ 803), her helplessness evokes
pity. At _Antigone_ 91, however, Antigone seems to echo Tekmessa: "Well, then, I shall cease (_pepausomai_) when my strength
fails." But the final word, _pepausomai_, literally, "I shall
have stopped myself,"[9] gives the whole line an ominous tone.
In a veiled way, she is announcing her suicide. She asks for
no advice or protection. Instead, like Ajax, she is ready for
the knife or noose.

But does not Antigone evoke pity in her long lament (806-82)
and final words (891-943) before she is led off to the rock-
hewn prison? It is then that all her pent-up emotions erupt as
she laments the bitter toll her act is costing her, crying out
for the joys of marriage, children, and daily life in her

native Thebes. Then, too, she speaks those twenty lines that
so embarrass modern commentators that they try to deny Sophocles wrote them;[10] in this passage, she loses sight of the unwritten laws of Zeus and the connection between these laws and
her act. She thus seems to contradict her earlier eloquent
defense of the agrapta nomina, "the unwritten laws" (450-70),
as she momentarily reduces her motivation to a sophistic
rationalism. She buried her brother, she now contends, not
because of a deep connection between philia (family love) and
the agrapta nomima as she asserted earlier, but because, with
her parents both dead, she could never have another brother
(905 ff.). But three things about this strange passage keep
her from becoming the object of pity in the way Ajax's wife
is. First, although she loses her clarity of vision, she never
recants, never once questions the rectitude of her act. If the
connection between human love and Zeus' law momentarily escapes
her, she does not lose faith in human love. Second, she does
not turn to the Chorus for help, nor does it presume to offer
her any (929-30). And finally, her irrationalism lasts only a
moment, as her last words quoted below (937-43) indicate.

Her lamentation, then, is informed by her religious instinct, and this instinct, both here and elsewhere, is "feminine" in that it proceeds from the concrete needs of one she
loves to the universal--and not vice versa. In her masterly
defense of the unwritten laws (450-70), she perceived that her
burial of Polynices was an act based on the universal and unqualified validity of the divine laws (452-53). But, even
then, she understood the validity of these laws in terms of
concrete, human needs: "But if I had left my mother's dead
son an unburied corpse, that would have grieved me" (466-67).
A fortiori, in her final speech when death is imminent and the
very gods seem to have deserted her (921), she has to make her
love of the corpse bear the total weight of her motivation.
She can do this without internal contradiction because her
religious instinct proceeds from the human to the transcendent,
rather than the other way around.

The last words Antigone speaks in the play (937-43) shows
she has regained both her earlier conviction of the religious

dimension of her act and, paradoxically, a sense of her autonomy: "O city of my fathers in the land of Thebes, O ancestral
gods! I am indeed led forth (agomai dē) and brook no more
delay. Observe the last daughter of the king's household. See
what I suffer--and from whose hands--because I revered reverence!"

Like Ajax, Antigone stands free and strong as she goes to
meet death. The Chorus, quite correctly if unwittingly,
earlier applied the Ajaxian epithets, autonomos, independent
(821), and autognōtos, self-willed (875), to her--and this it
did when her lament was most poignant and "feminine" in subject matter. But her autonomy is more limited than Ajax's.
He is convinced that he needs no help, not even from the gods
(Ajax 669, 749-77). Antigone's autonomy, on the contrary,
springs from her conviction that her nomos, guiding principle
or law, is one with the agrapta nomima (see Guide, chap. 4,
introduction to the "Defense of the Unwritten Laws"). So, in
the passage quoted above, there is an ambiguity in line 939
that expresses her religious conviction in typically cautious,
mysterious Sophoclean terms. When she says, "I am led forth,"
Creon would naturally understand her to mean "by the henchmen."
(The king always limits reality to things his eyes can see and
his henchmen are nearby waiting to take her away.) But she
does not express the agent and has just invoked the ancestral
gods. Furthermore, her very last phrase returns to them again:
"because I revered reverence." Such is Sophocles' understated
way with matters religious. An unambiguous statement of divine
action in a particular human situation is appropriate for
Shaw's Joan but not for a Sophoclean hero.[11] However, the clue
to her meaning is in the tiny particle dē (usually feebly
translated "indeed," but the word is at home in the great
moments of tragedy, as Denniston has remarked). "I am indeed
led forth (agomai dē)," she avers, but the power is that of
ancestral gods whose unwritten laws protect the dead.[12] Creon
does not understand. The audience perceives that she has regained her autonomy and dimly understands that there is a
connection between that autonomy and her reverence for reverence.

As a result, Antigone's grief is far too limited in scope
and her spirit is far too resilient for her to qualify as a
"supreme evoker of pity." Thomas Henn's phrase, with its
implicit condescension, does not apply to her anymore than it
does to Ajax.[13] The only pity Antigone elicits is the Aristo-
telian combination of "pity and terror" as defined by Stephen
Dedalus in a Portrait of the Artist: "pity is the feeling which
arrests the mind in the presence of whatsoever is grave and
constant in human sufferings and unites it with the human suf-
ferer. Terror is the feeling which arrests the mind in the
presence of whatsoever is grave and constant in human sufferings and unites it with the secret cause.[14] The audience
is united with Antigone's suffering and admires her courage.
However, concomitantly, it experiences the terror of being
confronted with her mysterious "secret cause."

Finally, I turn to some strikingly androgynous phrases in
the Prologue and some related images in the Ode on Man. I do
not, however, mean to infer that Sophocles was consciously
endowing Antigone with "masculine" and "feminine" traits. A
playwright does not create a character as one would mix ingre-
dients in a cake.

Antigone gives us the first of these phrases when she
declares her decision to bury Polynices: "I shall rest with him
faithful to his love, after performing the holy crime" (73-74).
In the phrase, "performing the holy crime" (hosia panour-
gēsas'), she displays "masculine" temerity and directness and
"feminine" love. Panourgein, to do anything and everything
necessary,[15] combines within itself the directness of a
straight line and the flexibility of a curve. The first half
of the word, pan (all, every), allows for any detours necessary. The second half, ergein (to do the deed), is straight
and direct. She will take a detour around the legally valid
edict of Creon and knows intuitively that such a "crime" is an
act of love, in both the human and divine sphere.

This declaration separates her from Ajax in that she puts
her enormous self-possession at the service of another. Simone
de Beauvoir regrets that women generally lack the forgetfulness
of self necessary for true greatness.[16] In Sophocles' Ajax and

Antigone, it is Ajax, I submit, who lacks the androgynous
wholeness to transcend his selfish glory. Antigone, like Ajax,
revels in the glory of her act (502-3), but her glory is
primarily altruistic,[17] not self-serving. Ajax's loving wife,
Tekmessa, muses that he died "to please himself" (_Ajax_ 967);
Antigone's primary motive is "to please those I most must
please" (89). And so, she is ready to play the criminal fool,
for a dead man's sake. Homeric _kleos_, glory, has been bent
into an act of love.

Ismene is the phrasemaker for the other androgynous phrases
in the Prologue. I underline the pertinent phrases below
(88-93).

> IS. Your heart is <u>hot for chilling deeds</u>.
>
> AN. Well, I know I please those I most should
>   please.
>
> IS. Yes, if you have the strength. <u>But you
>   are in love (erais) with the impossible
>   (amēchanon)</u>.
>
> AN. Well, then, I shall cease when I shall
>   have no more strength.
>
> IS. Oh, but it is not proper <u>to hunt for
>   impossibilities (ta amēchana)</u>.

In all of these phrases, there is a blending of opposites:[18]
passion blends with cold deeds, eros with unattainable loves,
hunting with unattainable prey. Hunting is the "masculine"
activity par excellence as the first antistrophe of the Ode on
Man (332 ff.) illustrates. Passionate loving (the verb _erāis_
is related to _eros_) is that fearful female activity that the
Greek male so feared and whose role in the drama becomes apparent in the Ode on Eros (781 ff.). And the object of both Antigone's passion (90) and her hunt (92) is _ta amēchana_, the realm
of the impossible; i.e., the arena into which optimistic Periclean man, confident in himself and his culture, thought he
could break (see Ode on Man and _Guide_, note on line 363). And
so, in effect, Ismene is calling Antigone back from the hori-
zons that the Ode on Man (332 ff.) is to proclaim. The chief
themes of the ode are present in Ismene's words: man's daring,
his hunting, his subjugating of forces thought to be beyond his

control. What is different is the perspective: Ismene speaks
as a frightened girl who would protect another little girl from
the consequences of her own strength. She lacks the Chorus's
confidence and joy in the deins anthrōpos (332-33), the
strangely wonderful person who is the subject of the ode.

We turn then to the ode for evidence that the poet, using
the Chorus as his ironic persona,[19] is on one level describing
androgynous heroism in its own generalizing terms. The "masculine" aspects of the ode are clearly evident; by concentrating
here on the less apparent "feminine" dimension, I suggest that
the ode may contain the poet's veiled warning to his civilization for its excessive "masculinity" and his hint that the
culprit about to be led on stage is really a deinos anthrōpos.

The first strophe and antistrophe hail "masculine" prowess
and male accomplismments. Although anthrōpos, the generic
word for mankind, is the subject of the ode, this Chorus of
Theban elders instinctively limits its song to male triumphs.
The first antistrophe makes the limitation explicit by chang-
ing the subject from anthrōpos to anēr, the male (342). The
imagery of yokes, nets, and curbs vividly expresses the male's
mastery as hunter, subjugator, and darer of impossible feats.

The second strophe shifts to the arena of the mind. The
Chorus sings of man's capacity for inner control, his suc-
cesses in internal feats and in communal endeavors. It is
here that "feminine" images dominate. I mention two: kai
phthegma kai ānemoen phronēma kai astynomous orgās, "language
and wind-swift thought and the temper that regulates communal
life" (354-55) and the weaving image of the final antistrophe
(368-69).

The yoke words have disappeared. Force is no longer an
appropriate tool. Wind-swift or high-soaring (ānemoen)
thought is man's proper instrument. The "high-soaring" suggests the bird imagery elsewhere associated with Antigone
(424-25) and with the other victims of male aggression (337-
38, 342-52); it also suggests the high ethical plane Antigone
has chosen.

The phrase, astynomous orgās, connotes the feeling or temper as well as the social impulse drawing people together into

a communal unit (see Guide,note on line 355). Thus the phrase
has a breadth that translators often miss. It does not connote
"statecraft," a narrowly male preserve in Periclean Athens, but
the wholly human or androgynous disposition that makes social
life possible. The grim Ajax is great precisely in his solitary stance against the needs of the community. His principle
is ōmos, savage, a word that is the strongest Greek antonym of
"civilized." He is the last exemplar of the individualistic
ethos. Antigone's principle, on the other hand, makes her not
ōmos but hypsipolis, "high in the city" (370), because her
guiding principle, philia, can by extension, preserve life in
society. Thus, the individualistic ethos gives way to one
appropriate for the polis.
  Finally, the second antistrophe introduces a startling
image taken from the life of woman in conscious contrast with
the male images of the first half of the ode: "Man possesses a
shrewd inventive genius beyond expectation--yet he comes now
to evil and now to good. But if he weaves (pareirōn) the laws
of the land in with the justice of the gods to whom oath binds
him, he stands high in the city (hypsipolis)" (365-70). The
Chorus here is admitting that the male prowess that it has
identified with civilization may ultimately destroy that very
civilization unless there is a "weaving in" of the divine and
human into society's fabric. The "weaving" image is so sur-
prising here that editors have almost universally emended the
text (see Guide, note on line 368). But the poet here is
consciously inserting this abrupt metaphor. It would seem that
he is implying the need for a "feminine" dimension in man if
his progress is to avoid moral bankruptcy (366-67). There must
be a harmony between the hunter, darer, and subjugator on the
one side, and the ardent lover of impossibilities, the lover
who finds glory in the service of others, on the other side.
  The dominance of "feminine" images in the second half of
the ode brings to the surface "feminine" elements in the first
strophe. I mention one:[20] the "feminine" dimension of deinos
and of the whole first line polla ta deina kouden anthrōpou
deinoteron pelei, "Wonders are many and nothing is more wondrously strange than man," with its recollections of the ini-

tial line of the central Ode of Aeschylus' Oresteia: Polla men
gā trephei deina deimatōn achē, "The Earth breeds many dis-
tressful things of terror" (Aeschylus Choephoroi 585-86). The
Aeschylean Chorus sings of the fearful sexual violence, un-
faithfulness, and superiority of the primitive female. The
eventual subjugation and constructive control of the savage
forces of woman by man's rational forces and the eventual
integration of both into the life of the polis are a dominant
theme of the whole Oresteia. To deinon in the Oresteia is that
female fearful passion personified in the Furies. The similarity in the openings of both odes is not accidental: Sophocles wants to remind his audience of the female meaning of to
deinon in Aeschylus' ode where the pre-Olympian, chthonic,
nonrational female deities are pitted against Apollo and the
rational male Olympians. Sophocles wants to recall, too,
Aeschylus' solution by which Athena, the sexually ambigious,
motherless daughter of Zeus, integrates the male and female
into the very life of the polis. But the younger poet then
takes that integration a step further. He seeks to incor-
porate the "masculine" and "feminine" into the very character of the hero. This "balanced poise" in the character of
Antigone makes her a deinos anthrōpos, a "wonder of mankind."

I have tried to show, then, that Antigone is an androgynous
heroine. She is this not because she has strong "masculine"
qualities and submissive "womanly" traits; and not even because
she has all the strong "masculine" qualities and all the strong
"feminine" qualities; but rather because she possesses a wholeness of character that weaves together some "masculine"
strengths and some "feminine" strengths into a glorious, although imperfect, unity. She exhibits Ajax's scandalous lib-
erty, his conviction, and the strength to affirm this conviction by suicide; she shares his concern for Homeric glory; and
her active attitude toward grief and death elicits Aristote-
lian pity rather than the pity of condescension. On the "feminine" side, she and Ajax both possess "deinotic" excess, the
passion to set conviction on fire; her passion, however, is
directed to the "feminine" act of love rather than the Ajaxian,
"masculine" act of war; her tenderness toward her loved ones

makes her "high in the city" rather than the "savage" destroyer
of the social fabric; finally, her logic and her religious
sense are both "feminine" in proceeding from the concrete needs
of her loved ones rather than from the universal to the concrete. The resulting androgyny makes it possible for the
heroine so to forget herself as to put her personal glory at
the service of a greater goal.

     She is not, however, a bloodless ideal. There is an uneven-
ness about her androgyny: Ismene, after the opening lines of
the play, Creon, and Haemon experience nothing of her tenderness, let alone gentleness; and she seems incapable of any
compromise. Indeed, after her early break with Ismene, she
reserves all her gentleness for the dead--a fact that accounts
for her apparent priggish arrogance. So, if the androgynous
ideal is to be "both assertive...and yielding, independent,
job- and people-oriented, strong and gentle,"[21] Antigone's
androgyny is hardly perfect. However, such unevenness makes
her character psychologically believable. In fact, psychologist Daniel Levinson observes that the growth of complementary
"masculine" and "feminine" qualities in an individual is inevi-
tably uneven, with one side lagging behind the other and the
ability to integrate them developing last.[22]

                    HAEMON'S GYNECANDRISM

     If Antigone is androgynous in such a way that her "mascu-
line" qualities obscure her "femininity," her fiancé, Haemon,
exemplifies a different kind of androgyny. In him, the "feminine" qualities are more readily apparent but they conceal a
strength of will, a decisiveness, a reasonableness that are
traditionally considered "masculine" traits. Thus, I invert
the word, "androgyny" and coin the word "gynecandrism" in order
to describe the kind of balance in Haemon's androgyny. An
examination of his brief role in the play will reveal his
gynecandrism and the complementarity of the ill-fated lovers.
By dramatizing their complementary natures in separate scenes,
without ever portraying their interaction (they have no scene
together), the poet was able to suggest the relationship they

might have achieved without sacrificing his greater goal, his
heroine's isolation from any human support.

The movement in the Third Episode from Haemon's submissive
first words to his ultimate rejection of his father's tyranny
is not a victory of his erotic impulses, as the Chorus thinks
(see the Ode on Eros, 781 ff.), but is consistent with his
gynecandrous nature. He begins with an admission, quite
appropriate for a Greek son but extraordinary to the modern
audience: "Father, I am yours. And when you guide well, you
set a straight path for me...and I for one shall follow it.
For I shall value no marriage more highly than your good guidance" (635-36). His last words can also mean "than your judgment when it is good." Only an astute audience would observe
the clever manipulation of language by which he supports his
father's good judgment but reserves his own right to decide
the parameters of good judgment. Haemon shares Ismene's
deference to superiors, but he stops short of her unqualified
submission (63). He does not ultimately submit in judgment or
action either to Creon or to Antigone. His independence
clearly separates him from accepted "feminine" behavior and
leads him by a less direct route to the same goal as Antigone.

Yet there is an accommodating openness and a touching
naïveté (traditionally "feminine" traits) in Haemon's reverence
for his father. These are evident in his unquestioning faith
in the power of reason: he proceeds as if sure that his father
will respond rationally to the justice and logic of his argument; he proceeds, too, as though sure that the autocratic
king will come to accept his own democratic conception of law
as the consensus of the people.[23] Haemon feels sure the king
will acknowledge his error once he understands that the people
support Antigone and that they are right in so doing.

The arguments and metaphors with which he tries to move his
father show how he accomodates himself to the king's frame of
reference. Creon loves aphorisms. Haemon talks in aphorisms.
His father can only understand the evidence of his senses.
The son bases his arguments on perceptible objects. Creon has
a hierarchical caste of mind. Haemon pays him every respect
possible and never directly mentions Antigone's rights or his

own love for her.

The images Haemon uses are from his father's storehouse:
the army, the ship of state, the storm at sea. The care with
which he chooses metaphor and argument shows the depth of his
concern for his father (741).[24] And the elaborate series of
metaphors all lead up to his climactic plea: "Yield! Let your
anger abate!" (718).[25] Thus, the role he assumes as he
cajoles, listens, urges, and compliments his father is altogether expressive of the "feminine" aspect of his personality
and is a calculated accommodation to his father's perceived
needs. But the very calculation and the reliance on reason,
not emotion, are "masculine" elements.

We have noted that Sophocles does not dramatize the relationship between Antigone and Haemon by a love scene or even a
word of love.[26] Yet, he does intimate what their relationship
might have become through the character portrayal of each in
encounters with third parties. Antigone and Haemon share
certain basic prerequisites for a strong relationship: both
are strong, sincere characters, capable of true compassion,
firm in adherence to principle, and exhibiting a healthy mix-
ture, although in different proportion, of "masculine" and
"feminine" virtues. Beyond those basic similarities, they
could not be more different: her language is stern, usually
"masculine" in its dearth of metaphor, though the subjects she
treats are "feminine," and her emotions are always close to the
surface. His language is warm, gentle, and metaphoric, though
he relies on logic rather than passion. He tends to listen,
where she tends to make pronouncements. He searches for
common ground; her uncompromising approach breeds confrontation.[27]

Antigone's decision of love leads her to a cold rejection
of the "enemy," whether Creon or Ismene; at the beginning of
the Third Episode, Haemon is still open to the two great loves
of his young life, refusing to view Creon as "enemy" as Antigone would, and refusing to reject Antigone as his father
would. He would bend, as he urges his father to do, until
finally, with all the evidence in, both his independent judgment and his passionate love lead him to realize that the

value system that he shares with Antigone is incompatible with
that of his father (743-46).[28]

Only one line in the play alludes to the complementarity of
Antigone and Haemon. It is a line in the Second Episode (570),
where Ismene and Creon are debating as Antigone listens.

> IS. Will you kill your own son's fiancee?
>
> CR. There are other fields for him to
> plow.
>
> IS. Not in a union so close (hērmosmena)
> as his and hers.
>
> CR. I hate evil wives for my sons.
>
> IS. Oh dearest Haemon, how your father
> dishonors you.

These lines (568-72) have caused much scholarly disagreement,
especially since some modern critics and editors have given
the last line (572) to Antigone, rather than to Ismene as the
manuscript tradition does. While I reject the emendation and
the romanticism that prompted it,[29] I wish to focus attention
here on Ismene's previous statement (570). She uses hērmos-
mena, "harmoniously fit," to describe the relationship of
Haemon and her sister. Harmozdein, suggesting a musical metaphor,[30] implies a harmonious balance that exceeds prevailing
Greek custom between the sexes. Naturally, Ismene would realize that her headstrong sister could only find happiness in a
relationship that respected her autonomy. The excessive anger
that vibrates in Creon's reply suggests that he caught
Ismene's implication.

The daughter of Oedipus, harsh in the eyes of the Chorus
(471) and example of the deinos anthrōpos (323 ff.), would not
be a comfortable wife for any Greek, whether in the heroic age
or even less in Periclean Athens.[31] Yet, despite Haemon's
undervaluation of marriage (from a modern perspective) in comparison with filial duties, his mature concern, his quiet
restraint, and his reasonable, conciliatory nature make it a
fair assumption that he, if anyone, would be a fitting gynecandrous counterpart for Antigone. It is part of the tragedy
that this androgynous couple can find union only in the harbor
of Hades (1284).

THE GREEK ALPHABET

	PRONUNCIATION	TRANSLITERATION	NAMES OF LETTERS
α	As first a in <u>aha</u>	a	alpha
ᾱ	As a in English <u>father</u>	ā	
ᾳ	As ᾱ	ai	
αι	As in English <u>high</u>	ai, ae	
αυ	As in English <u>how</u>	au	
β	As English <u>b</u>	b	bēta
γ	1) As English "hard" g 2) Before γ,κ,ξ,χ as <u>n</u> in English <u>think</u>	g n	gamma
δ	As English <u>d</u>	d	delta
ε	As in English <u>pet</u>	e	epsīlon
ει	As in English <u>freight</u>	ei	
ευ	A glide from ε toward υ	eu	
ζ	<u>Zd</u> as in English <u>wisdom</u>*	zd, dz	zeta
η	As in English <u>they</u>	ē	ēta
ῃ	As <u>ēta</u>	ēi	
ηυ	As ευ	ēu	

*See W. Sidney Allen, <u>Vox Graeca</u> (Cambridge: Cambridge Univ. Press, 1968), pp. 53-54, where Allen gives convincing evidence that zd not dz is the proper transliteration. This list has been taken with some adaptation from Allen, pp. 155-57.

	PRONUNCIATION	TRANSLITERATION	NAMES OF LETTERS
ϑ	As in English <u>top</u> (emphatically pronounced)	th	thēta
ι	As in English <u>bit</u>	i	iōta
ῑ	As in French <u>vive</u>	ī	
κ	As English <u>k</u> or "hard" <u>c</u>	k, c	kappa
λ	As English <u>l</u>	l	lambda
μ	As English <u>m</u>	m	mū
ν	As English <u>n</u>	n	nū
ξ	As <u>x</u> in English <u>box</u>	x	xī
ο	As in English <u>pot</u>	o	omīcron
οι	As in English <u>boy</u>	oi	
ου	As in English <u>pool</u>	ou	
π	As English (noninitial) <u>p</u>	p	pī
ρ	As Scottish rolled <u>r</u>	r, rh (initial)	rhō
σ,ς	As <u>s</u> in English <u>sing</u>, or <u>ss</u> in less	s	sigma
τ	As English (noninitial) <u>t</u>	t	tau
υ	As in French <u>lune</u>	u	upsīlon
ῡ	As in French <u>ruse</u>	ū	
φ	As <u>p</u> in English <u>pot</u> (emphatically pronounced)	ph	phī
χ	As <u>ch</u> in Scottish <u>loch</u>	ch	chī
ψ	As <u>ps</u> in English <u>lapse</u>	ps	psī
ω	ō	ō	ōmega
ῳ	As <u>ōmega</u>	ōi	

ASPIRATION

The aspirate in Greek early lost the symbol H. Instead, an initial aspirate, roughly equivalent to our h sound, is expressed by a superscript |'|, called a "rough breathing." Later, a corresponding superscript |'|, called a "smooth breathing," was introduced to indicate nonaspiration. Thus, words beginning with a vowel have either a rough or a smooth breathing. A word with a rough breathing is transliterated with an initial h; such a word, e.g., haima, "blood," is listed in the "Vocabulary" (chap. 8 in the Guide) under the initial vowel, in this case under the letter a. Aspiration is also included in some letters; e.g., letters phī, thēta, and chī are the aspirated forms of pī, tau, and kappa.

NASALS

In addition to the two letters, mū and nū, a third nasal having the sound of n (as in think or sing) does not have a separate symbol. It is represented in Greek by a gamma. A gamma before a kappa, chī, xī, or another gamma is this third nasal and thus is transliterated as n: e.g., pankakistos, engenes, and tynchanō all include a gamma in the Greek.

BILINGUAL

SELECTIONS

FROM

SOPHOCLES'

ANTIGONE

DRAMATIS PERSONAE

DRAMATIS PERSONAE

Antigone   (An teé gon ne),   daughter of Oedipus and Jocasta, also sister to Oedipus

Ismene   (Is meé ne),   sister of Antigone

Creon   (Kreé on),   king of Thebes, brother of Jocasta

Haemon   (Heé mon or Haý mon),   son of Creon, fiancé of Antigone

Guard

Tiresias   (Tai reé si as),   the prophet of Thebes

Messenger or messengers

Eurydice   (You rí di se),   wife of Creon, mother of Haemon and Megareus (Menoeceus)

Chorus of Theban elders, represented in the dialogue portions by the Chorus Leader

I

The Prologue and

the Parodos

THE SETTING

In the partial light of predawn, Antigone comes out of the Women's Quarters of the royal palace of Thebes leading her sister Ismene by the hand. It is the day after the death of their two brothers, slain each by the other's hand, Eteocles while defending Thebes, Polynices while leading the Argive army against the city. Oedipus, their father, had put a curse of mutual slaughter upon the two.

The huge theatre of Dionysos, empty except for its altar, dwarfs the two young girls. The spectacle thus heightens the viewer's perception that these sisters who run down the long parodos onto the massive circular orchestra have only each other for support, now that word of the king's decree con- demning their traitorous brother has incensed and alienated Antigone. Her opening words confirm her sense of isolation and her highly charged emotional state.

2

The Prologue and the Parodos

THE PROLOGUE, 1-99

ΑΝΤΙΓΟΝΗ   ANTIGONĒ

Ὦ	κοινὸν		αὐτάδελφον	Ἰσμήνης	κάρα,
Ō	koinon		autadelphon	Ismēnēs	karā,
O	kindred, of common parents, interests		own-sister	Ismene	head = dear

ἆρ'	οἶσθ'	ὅ τι	Ζεὺς τῶν	ἀπ'	Οἰδίπου κακῶν
ar(a)	oisth(a)	ho ti	Zeus tōn	ap(o)	Oidipou kakōn
	do you know	whatever	Zeus of the	from	Oedipus ills, evils

ὁποῖον	οὐχὶ	νῷν	ἔτι	ζώσαιν	τελεῖ;
hopoion	ouchi	nōin	eti	dzōsain	telei?
such as, what	not	us two	still	living even during our lifetime	he will fulfill

οὐδὲν	γὰρ	οὔτ'	ἀλγεινὸν	οὔτ'	ἄτης	ἄτερ
ouden	gar	out(e)	algeinon	out(e)	atēs	ater
nothing	for	neither	painful	nor	calamity, ruin	without, free from

οὔτ'	αἰσχρὸν	οὔτ'	ἄτιμόν	ἔσθ',	ὁποῖον οὐ	5
out(e)	aischron	out(e)	atīmon	est(i),	hopoion ou	
nor	(morally) shameful	nor	dishonorable	is there	of what sort	

τῶν	σῶν	τε	κἀμῶν	οὐκ	ὄπωπ'	ἐγὼ κακῶν.
tōn	sōn	te	ka(i)(e)mōn	ouk	opōp(a)	egō kakōn.
of the	your	both	and my	not	I have seen	I evils

καὶ νῦν	τί	τοῦτ'	αὖ	φασι	πανδήμῳ	πόλει
kai nȳn	ti	tout(o)	au	phasi	pandēmōi	polei
and now	what	this	anew	they say	public, belonging to all the people	city

κήρυγμα	θεῖναι	τὸν	στρατηγὸν	ἀρτίως;
kērygma	theinai	ton	stratēgon	artiōs?
proclamation, spoken edict	make	the	general	lately, recently

ἔχεις	τι	κε(σ)ήκουσας;	ἤ	σε	λανθάνει
echeis	ti	k(ai) eisēkousas? ē	se	lanthanei
do you know	anything	and have you heard or	you	does it escape

πρὸς	τοὺς	φίλους	στείχοντα	τῶν ἐχθρῶν	κακά; 10
pros	tous	philous	steichonta	tōn echthrōn	kaka?
upon	the (our)	one's own, relatives, loved ones	advancing	of the enemies, from enemies	evils

ΙΣΜΗΝΗ   ISMĒNĒ

ἐμοὶ	μὲν	οὐδεὶς	μῦθος,	᾿Αντιγόνη,	φίλων
emoi	men	oudeis	mȳthos,	Antigonē,	philōn
to me	no	word		Antigone	about dear ones, with respect to loved ones

οὔθ᾿	ἡδὺς	οὔτ᾿	ἀλγεινὸς	ἵκετ᾿	ἐξ	ὅτου
out(e)	hēdys	out(e)	algeinos	hīket(o)	ex	hotou
neither	sweet, welcome	nor	painful	has come, has reached (me)	from	which time, from the time when

δυοῖν	ἀδελφοῖν	ἐστερήθημεν	δύο,
dyoin	adelphoin	esterēthēmen	dyo,
of two	brothers	we were robbed	two

AN. Ismene, my own, my very dear sister, do you know, are there any ills inherited from Oedipus that Zeus will not fulfill in us two survivors? For there is nothing painful or calamitous, shameful or dishonorable that I have not seen in your woes and mine. And now what is this new edict that they say the general has just published to the whole of Thebes? Do you know anything about it? Have you heard? Or are you unaware of the enemies' evil plots marching against those we love?

IS. No, Antigone, no word about our loved ones, either sweet or painful, has reached me from the moment we two were robbed of our two brothers

μιᾷ   θανόντοιν   ἡμέρᾳ   διπλῇ   χερί·
miāi   thanontoin   hēmerāi diplēi   cheri;
on one   slain,   day   by a twofold right hand
           put to death   (i.e., each by the other's hand)

ἐπεὶ   δε   φροῦδός   ἐστιν   Ἀργείων   στρατὸς   15
epei   de   phroudos   estin   Argeiōn   stratos
since and   fled away   of the Argives   army

ἐν   νυκτὶ   τῇ   νῦν,   οὐδὲν   οἶδ·   ὑπέρτερον,
en   nykti   tēi   nȳn,   ouden   oid(a) hyperteron,
in   the night the   now   nothing I know more, further
                     (i.e., just now,
                     just past)

οὔτ·   εὐτυχοῦσα   μᾶλλον   οὔτ·   ἀτωμένη.
out(e)   eutychousa   māllon   out(e)   atōmenē.
neither   being fortunate more   nor   being in trouble,
                                              suffering

AN. ἤδη   καλῶς,   καί σ·   ἐκτὸς   αὐλείων   πυλῶν
    ēidē   kalōs,   kai s(e) ektos   auleiōn   pylōn
    I knew well   and you   outside of court,   gate,
                                          of outer door   housedoor

    τοῦδ·   οὕνεκ·   ἐξέπεμπον,   ὡς   μόνη   κλύοις.
    toud(e) hounek(a)   exepempon,   hōs   monē   klyois.
    this   because of I was leading out,   so that alone you might
                        was calling outside   hear

ΙΣ. τί   δ·   ἐστι;   δηλοῖς   γάρ τι   καλχαίνουσ·   ἔπος.   20
    ti   d(e) esti?   dēlois   gar ti   kalchainous(a) epos.
    what   is it   you are for some making purple, word,
                      plainly   brooding   news

AN. οὐ   γὰρ   τάφου   νῷν   τὼ   κασιγνήτω   Κρέων
    ou   gar   taphou   nōin tō   kasignētō   Kreōn
    not why   of a tomb,   our   the   brothers   Creon
               of burial

τὸν   μὲν   προτίσας,   τὸν   δ'   ἀτιμάσας   ἔχει;
ton   men   protīsās,   ton   d(e)   atīmasās   echei?
the   one   preferred in   the   other dishonored   does he hold
             honor   himself, is he

'Ετεοκλέα   μέν,   ὡς   λέγουσι,   σὺν   δίκῃ
Eteoklea   men,   hōs   legousi,   syn   dikēi
Eteocles   on the one hand   as   they say   with   justice

χρησθεὶς   δικαίᾳ   καὶ   νόμῳ,   κατὰ   χθονὸς
chrēstheis   dikaiāi   kai   nomōi,   kata   chthonos
treating,   righteous   and   usage,   funeral   under the ground
having treated   rites

ἔκρυψε   τοῖς   ἔνερθεν   ἔντιμον   νεκροῖς,   25
ekrypse   tois   enerthen entīmon   nekrois,
he has buried among those below   honored,   dead
                                     holding honors

τὸν   δ'   ἀθλίως   θανόντα   Πολυνείκους   νέκυν
ton   d(e) athliōs   thanonta   Polyneikous   nekyn
the other but   wretchedly dying   of Polynices dead body

ἀστοῖσί   φασιν   ἐκκεκηρῦχθαι   τὸ   μὴ
astoisi   phāsin   ekkekērȳchthai   to   mē
to the citizens they say   to have been banished   the   not
                           by proclamation

when they killed each other in mutual fury on one day. And
since the departure this very night of the Argive army, I know
of no news good or bad.

     AN. I knew that and therefore I called you here outside
the gate so that you alone might hear.

     IS. What is it? You obviously are brooding on some dark
news.

     AN. Why, of course, has not Creon held one of our broth-
ers worthy of honorable burial and the other not? The report
is that he, properly observing justice and custom, has buried
Eteocles in the earth among the dead below; but that no one

τάφῳ   καλύψαι   μηδὲ   κωκῦσαί   τινα,
taphōi   kalypsai   mēde   kōkȳsai   tina,
in a tomb to cover   nor   to shriek over, lament   anyone

ἐᾶν   δ' ἄκλαυτον,   ἄταφον,   οἰωνοῖς γλυκὺν
eān   d(e) aklauton, ataphon, oiōnois glykyn
to leave but unwept   unburied for the sweet (to taste and
                                    birds   smell), welcome

θησαυρὸν εἰσορῶσι   πρὸς χάριν   βορᾶς.   30
thēsauron eisorōsi   pros charin   borās.
store,   looking down on for gratification, of feeding,
treasure   as they will   of feasting

τοιαῦτά   φασι   τὸν ἀγαθὸν   Κρέοντα   σοὶ
toiauta   phāsi   ton agathon   Kreonta   soi
such   they say the good, worthy Creon   to you

κάμοί,   λέγω γὰρ κάμέ,   κηρύξαντ'   ἔχειν,
ka(i)(e)moi, legō gar ka(i)(e)me, kēryxant(a) echein,
and to me   I say yes also to me published   has

καὶ δεῦρο νεῖσθαι ταῦτα   τοῖσι   μὴ εἰδόσιν
kai deuro neisthai tauta   toisi   mē eidosin
and here   to come these (things)   for those   not knowing

σαφῆ   προκηρύξοντα,   καὶ τὸ   πρᾶγμ'   ἄγειν
saphē   prokēryxonta,   kai to   prāgm(a) agein
clearly   to proclaim   and the thing   to estimate,
                                               to consider

οὐχ ὡς παρ' οὐδέν,   ἀλλ' ὃς   ἂν τούτων τι δρᾷ,   35
ouch hōs par(a) ouden, all(a) hos   an toutōn ti drāi,
not as at   nothing but   whoever at all trans-
             of slight value   gresses

φόνον   προκεῖσθαι   δημόλευστον   ἐν πόλει.
phonon prokeisthai   dēmoleuston   en polei.
death   to be appointed by public stoning, by in the city
                       stoning of the people   publicly

οὕτως	ἔχει	σοι	ταῦτα,	καὶ δείξεις	τάχα
houtōs	echei	soi	tauta,	kai deixeis	tacha
thus	are	to you	these (things)	and you will show	speedily

εἴτ'	εὐγενὴς	πέφυκας	εἴτ'	ἐσθλῶν	κακή.
eit(e)	eugenēs	pephykas	eit(e)	esthlōn	kakē.
whether	nobly born, noble	you are by nature	or	of good, noble (parents)	ignoble, base

Σ.
τί	δ'	ὦ ταλαῖφρον,	εἰ τάδ'	ἐν τούτοις,	ἐγὼ
ti	d(e)	ō talaiphron,	ei tad(e)	en toutois,	egō
what	but	O much enduring (one)	if those (things)	in these (circumstances)	I

λύουσ'	ἂν εἴθ'	ἅπτουσα	προσθείμην	πλέον;	40
lyous(a)	an eit(e)	haptousa	prostheimēn	pleon?	
loosening, breaking	or	making fast (a knot), observing	might I bring further help	more (for your benefit)	

Ν.
εἰ	ξυμπονήσεις	καὶ ξυνεργάσῃ	σκόπει.
ei	xymponēseis	kai xynergasei	skopei.
whether	you will toil with, collaborate	and you will help in accomplishing	consider

may bury or mourn the wretched corpse of Polynices. Such is
Creon's decree to the townspeople. Instead, they must leave it
unwept, unburied, a welcome prize for birds on the lookout for
a feast. Such they say is the edict the good Creon has published for you and me--yes, even for me--and they say he is
coming here to proclaim this in case anyone is uninformed.
Furthermore, he judges the matter of such importance that any
transgressor shall be publicly stoned to death before the
assembled populace. That's it, then. And soon you will show
whether you are really noble, or whether you are a base daughter of noble parents.

IS. But if things are so, poor sister, what help or hin-
drance could I be by act or omission?

AN. Decide whether you will collaborate and share the
accomplishment.

ΙΣ. ποῖόν   τι κινδύνευμα;   ποῦ   γνώμης   ποτ'   εἶ;
    poion   ti kindyneuma?   pou   gnōmēs   pot(e) ei?
    what kind of   hazard, venture   where in thought ever   are you
                                       (what can you be thinking of?)

ΑΝ. εἰ   τὸν   νεκρὸν   ξὺν   τῇδε   κουφιεῖς   χερί.
    ei   ton   nekron   xyn   tēide   kouphieis   cheri.
    whether   the   corpse   together with this   you will   hand
                                        (i.e., my)   lift up

ΙΣ. ἦ   γὰρ   νοεῖς   θάπτειν   σφ',   ἀπόρρητον   πόλει;
    ē   gar   noeis   thaptein   sph(e) aporrhēton   polei?
    in truth   what! do you   to bury   him   forbidden   to the
                 why!   intend   city

ΑΝ. τὸν   γοῦν   ἐμὸν   καὶ   τὸν   σόν,   ἦν σὺ   μὴ   θέλῃς,   45
    ton   goun   emon   kai   ton   son,   ēn sy   mē   theleis,
          at any my   and   your   if you not should consent,
          rate   be willing

    ἀδελφόν·   οὐ   γὰρ   δὴ   προδοῦσ'   ἁλώσομαι.
    adelphon;   ou   gar   dē   prodous(a) halōsomai.
    brother   not   for   now   betraying   I shall be caught,
                                                I shall be found

ΙΣ. ὦ   σχετλία,   Κρέοντος   ἀντειρηκότος;
    ō   schetliā,   Kreontos   anteirēkotos?
    O   daring, headstrong,   Creon   forbidding
          wretched fool   (i.e., when, although Creon forbids)

ΑΝ. ἀλλ'   οὐδὲν   αὐτῷ   τῶν ἐμῶν   μ'   εἴργειν   μέτα.
    all(a)   ouden   autōi   tōn emōn   m(e)   eirgein   meta.
    but   not at   to him (from) me   to bar there is claim,
             all   my own   there is right

ΙΣ. οἴμοι·   φρόνησον,   ὦ   κασιγνήτη,   πατὴρ
    oimoi;   phronēson,   ō   kasignētē,   patēr
    alas!   think   O   sister   father

ὡς	νῦν	ἀπεχθὴς	δυσκλεής	τ᾽	ἀπώλετο,	50
hōs	noin	apechthēs	dyskleēs	t(e)	apōleto,	
how	us	detested	infamous	and	he died, he perished	

πρὸς	αὐτοφώρων	ἀμπλακημάτων	διπλᾶς
pros	autophōrōn	amplakēmatōn	diplās
in consequence of	self-detected, brought to light by his own search	errors	both

ὄψεις	ἀράξας	αὐτὸς	αὐτουργῷ	χερί˙
opseis	araxās	autos	autourgōi	cheri;
eyes	having torn out	he himself, by his own act	with (hand) against oneself	hand

ἔπειτα	μήτηρ	καὶ	γυνή,	διπλοῦν	ἔπος,
epeita	mētēr	kai	gynē,	diploun	epos,
then	mother	and	wife	double, twofold	word, name, designation

πλεκταῖσιν	ἀρτάναισι	λωβᾶται	βίον˙
plektaisin	artanaisi	lōbātai	bion;
with twisted	nooses, halters	ends disgracefully, destroys	life

IS. In what kind of venture? What are you planning?

AN. Will you share in burying the corpse?

IS. What? You intend to bury him despite the prohibition to the whole city?

AN. My brother I shall bury and yours too, if you will not. I shall not be found his traitor.

IS. O foolish sister! Even despite Creon?

AN. He has no right to keep me from my own.

IS. Alas, sister! Remember how our father perished detested and infamous, how he searched out his own sins and then tore out both eyes with his own hands, then how his mother-wife (dual title) endured the disgraceful death by a twisted noose.

τρίτον   δ'   ἀδελφώ   δύο   μίαν   καθ'   ἡμέραν   55
triton   d(e)   adelphō̄   dyo   mian   kat(a)   hēmerān
thirdly   and   brothers   two   one   in   day

αὐτοκτονοῦντε   τὼ   ταλαιπώρω   μόρον
autoktonounte   tō̄   talaipōrō̄   moron
slaying with their own hands   hapless   fate

κοινὸν   κατειργάσαντ'   ἐπ'   ἀλλήλοιν   χεροῖν.
koinon   kateirgasant(o)   ep(i)   allēloin   cheroin.
common   they accomplished   by   one another's,   (violent)
                                       mutual   hands

νῦν   δ'   αὖ   μόνα   δὴ   νὼ   λελειμμένα   σκόπει
nȳn   d(e)   au   monā̄   dē̄   nō̄   leleimmena   skopei
now   but   in our   all   indeed   us   left   see,
              turn   alone   consider

ὅσῳ   κάκιστ'   ὀλούμεθ',   εἰ νόμου   βίᾳ
hosō̄i   kakist(a)   oloumeth(a),   ei nomou   biāi
by how   most miserably we shall die if   custom,   in spite of,
much   law   in violation of

ψῆφον   τυράννων   ἢ   κράτη   παρέξιμεν.   60
psēphon   tyrannō̄n   ē̄   kratē̄   pareximen.
pebble, vote,   of the rulers   or   powers   we shall violate,
decree, will   we shall transgress

ἀλλ'   ἐννοεῖν   χρὴ   τοῦτο μὲν   γυναῖχ'   ὅτι
all(a)   ennoein   chrē̄   touto men   gynaich(e)   hoti
but   to bear   it is   this   in the   women   that
       in mind   necessary   first place

ἔφυμεν,   ὡς   πρὸς   ἄνδρας   οὐ   μαχουμένα·
ephymen,   hōs   pros   andras   ou   machoumena;
we were born,   and thus   against   men   not   being fitted
we are by nature   to fight

ἔπειτα   δ'   οὕνεκ'   ἀρχόμεσθ',   ἐκ   κρεισσόνων
epeita   d(e)   hounek(a)   archomesth(a)   ek   kreissonō̄n
next   and   that   we are ruled   by   the stronger

καὶ	ταῦτ'		ἀκούειν	κἄτι		τῶνδ'	ἀλγίονα.
kai	taut(a)		akouein	ka(i)(e)ti		tōnd(e)	algiona.
and	(in regard to) these (things)		so as to obey	and still		(than) these	more painful

ἐγὼ	μὲν	οὖν	αἰτοῦσα	τοὺς	ὑπὸ	χθονὸς	65
egō	men	oun	aitousa	tous	hypo	chthonos	
I	indeed	therefore	asking	those	under	ground, the earth	

ξύγγνοιαν	ἴσχειν,	ὡς	βιάζομαι	τάδε,
xyngnoian	ischein,	hōs	biazdomai	tade,
excuse, mercy	to have	since	I am forced	in these (matters)

τοῖς	ἐν τέλει	βεβῶσι	πείσομαι.	τὸ γὰρ
tois	en telei	bebōsi	peisomai.	to gar
to those	in authority, power	to those being	I will yield, I will obey	for

περισσὰ	πράσσειν	οὐκ	ἔχει	νοῦν	οὐδένα.
perissa	prassein	ouk	echei	noun	oudena.
extreme (things) (meddling, being heroic)	doing, to do	not	has	sense (is not sensible)	no

N.	οὔτ'	ἂν	κελεύσαιμ'	οὔτ'	ἄν,	εἰ	θέλοις	ἔτι
	out(e)	an	keleusaim(i)	out(e)	an,	ei	thelois	eti
	and not		I would bid, urge	nor		if	you would consent	yet

And finally on a single day our two ill-fated brothers each
brought violent death to the other, a common fate by a mutual
slaughter. So look at us now, utterly alone. How much more
wretchedly we will die if we defy the will and authority of the
rulers. No, remember that we are women, unfit therefore to
fight against men; and also that since the rulers are stronger
than we, we must obey these commands and even more painful ones.
So I implore the spirits below for forgiveness, and under con-
straint I will obey those in authority. For meddling makes no
sense at all.

　　　　AN. I would not urge you, no,

πράσσειν,   ἐμοῦ γ᾽   ἂν   ἡδέως   δρῴης   μέτα.   70
prassein,   emou g(e) an   hēdeōs   drōiēs   meta.
to do, act   me for my   gladly, with you would   with
                 part   my consent   work

ἀλλ᾽   ἴσθ᾽   ὁποία   σοι   δοκεῖ,   κεῖνον δ᾽   ἐγὼ
all(a)   isth(i) hopoiā   soi   dokei,   keinon d(e) egō
but   be   such as to you it seems best   him   but I

θάψω.   καλόν   μοι   τοῦτο   ποιούσῃ   θανεῖν.
thapsō   kalon   moi   touto   poiousēi   thanein.
shall bury   good,   for me this   doing   to die, be
             noble   put to death

φίλη   μετ᾽   αὐτοῦ κείσομαι,   φίλου   μέτα,
philē   met(a) autou keisomai,   philou   meta,
dear, loved with   him   I shall lie (my) dear (one)   with

ὅσια   πανουργήσασ᾽·   ἐπεὶ   πλείων χρόνος
hosia   panourgēsās(a);   epei   pleiōn chronos
hallowed,   having played the knave,   since more,   time
sanctioned by having acted the rogue   longer
divine law

ὃν   δεῖ   μ᾽   ἀρέσκειν τοῖς κάτω   τῶν   ἐνθάδε.   75
hon   dei   m(e) areskein tois katō   tōn   enthade.
(during) it is   me   to   those below (than)   here
which   necessary   please   those

ἐκεῖ   γὰρ αἰεὶ   κείσομαι·   σοὶ   δ᾽   εἰ δοκεῖ,
ekei   gar aiei   keisomai;   soi   d(e) ei dokei,
there   for forever I shall lie for you, but   if it seems
                                    to you   best

τὰ   τῶν   θεῶν   ἔντιμ᾽   ἀτιμάσασ᾽   ἔχε.
ta   tōn   theōn   entīm(a)   atīmasās(a)   eche.
the   of the gods   honored (things) dishonored,   keep
                                           slighting

Σ. ἐγὼ   μὲν   οὐκ   ἄτιμα   ποιοῦμαι,   τὸ   δὲ
   egō   men   ouk   atīma   poioumai,   to   de
   I   not   dishonorable (things) do, consider   but

   βίᾳ   πολιτῶν   δρᾶν   ἔφυν   ἀμήχανος.
   biāi   polītōn   drān   ephyn   amēchanos.
   against the the citizens to act I am   powerless,
   will of   by nature incapable, unable

Ν. σὺ   μὲν   τάδ'   ἂν προύχοι''   ἐγὼ δὲ   δὴ   τάφον   80
   sy   men   tad(e)   an prouchoi(o); egō de   dē   taphon
   you for your these   may make   I   but now a tomb,
       part   (excuses)   excuses   mound

   χώσουσ'   ἀδελφῷ   φιλτάτῳ   πορεύσομαι.
   chōsous(a)   adelphōi   philtatōi   poreusomai.
   to raise,   (over my) brother dearest, own,   I shall go
   to heap up   very dear

Σ. οἴμοι,   ταλαίνης   ὡς   ὑπερδέδοικά   σου.
   oimoi,   talainēs   hōs   hyperdedoika   sou.
   alas   unhappy, daring, how   I fear exceedingly   for you
               wretched

I would not allow you to collaborate, if later you want to.
No, be as you will. I shall bury him. In so doing, I shall
die a noble death. I shall rest with him, faithful to his
love, having played the saintly villain. It is for a longer
time that I must please the dead than the living. For I shall
rest with them forever. But do as you wish, dishonor the
hallowed laws of the gods.
        IS. I do not dishonor them, but I am powerless to act
against the city's will.
        AN. Make your excuses. My next act is to raise a tomb
over my dear brother.
        IS. My poor sister, how I fear for you.

AN. μὴ   'μοῦ   προτάρβει· τὸν σὸν ἐξόρθου   πότμον.
    mē   (e)mou   protarbei; ton son exorthou   potmon.
    do   for me   fear, be   your   steer straight, fate, destiny
    not   anxious   own   make prosperous

ΙΣ. ἀλλ'   οὖν   προμηνύσῃς   γε   τοῦτο   μηδενὶ
    all(a) oun   promēnysēis ge   touto   mēdeni
    well   at any rate   reveal   at least   this   to no one

    τοὔργον,   κρυφῇ   δὲ κεῦθε, σὺν δ'   αὔτως   ἐγώ. 85
    to (e)rgon, kryphēi   de keuthe, syn d(e) autōs   egō.
    the deed   in secret but hide   also and likewise, I
                                               similarly

AN. οἴμοι,   καταύδα·   πολλὸν ἐχθίων   ἔσῃ
    oimoi,   katauda;   pollon echthiōn   esēi
    alas   denounce (it, me),   much   more hated you will be
             speak out plainly

    σιγῶσ',   ἐὰν   μὴ πᾶσι κηρύξῃς   τάδε.
    sīgōs(a),   ean   mē pāsi kēryxēis   tade.
    being silent   unless to all   you proclaim these (things)

ΙΣ. θερμὴν   ἐπὶ   ψυχροῖσι   καρδίαν   ἔχεις.
    thermēn   epi   psychroisi   kardiān   echeis.
    hot   for   chilling, cold (deeds)   heart   you have

AN. ἀλλ'   οἶδ'   ἀρέσκουσ'   οἷς μάλισθ'   ἀδεῖν   με χρή.
    all(a) oid(a) areskous(a) hois malist(a) hadein   me chrē.
    but,   I know pleasing   to   espe-   to please me it is
    well   whom cially   necessary

ΙΣ. εἰ   καὶ   δυνήσῃ   γ'·   ἀλλ'   ἀμηχάνων   ἐρᾷς.   90
    ei   kai   dynēsēi   g(e); all(a) amēchanōn   erāis.
    if   also, you will   indeed but   impossible you desire
         yes   be able   (things)   passionately,
                                                       you are in
                                                       love with

οὐκοῦν, ὅταν δὴ μὴ σθένω, πεπαύσομαι.
oukoun, hotan dē mē sthenō, pepausomai.
well then, as soon as, at last not I am strong I shall cease
no when

ἀρχὴν δὲ θηρᾶν οὐ πρέπει τἀμήχανα.
archēn de thērān ou prepei t(a) amēchana.
to begin with, but to hunt not it is proper the impossible
yes after

εἰ ταῦτα λέξεις, ἐχθαρῇ μὲν ἐξ ἐμοῦ,
ei tauta lexeis, echtharēi men ex emou,
if these you (will) say you will be from me
(things) hated for my part

ἐχθρὰ δὲ τῷ θανόντι προσκείσῃ δίκῃ.
echthrā de tōi thanonti proskeisēi dikēi.
hated, the dead (one) you will be attached to, justly
hostile brought into relationship with

ἀλλ' ἔα με καὶ τὴν ἐξ ἐμοῦ δυσβουλίαν 95
all(a) ea me kai tēn ex emou dysbouliān
but allow me and the (proceeding) from me folly

AN. Don't fear for me. Look to your own course.

IS. At least do not reveal the deed to anyone. Keep it secret and so will I.

AN. For heaven's sake, shout it forth! I shall hate you far more if you keep silent and do not proclaim the deed to all.

IS. Your heart is hot for chilling deeds.

AN. Well, I know I please those I most should please.

IS. Yes, if you have the strength. But you are in love with the impossible.

AN. Well, then, I shall cease when I shall have no more strength.

IS. But it is not proper to hunt for impossibilities.

AN. If this is your advice, I shall hate you and so will the dead--justly--forevermore. Let me and my folly

παθεῖν   τὸ   δεινὸν   τοῦτο·   πείσομαι   γὰρ   οὐ
pathein   to   deinon   touto;   peisomai   gar   ou
suffer,   the   fearful,   this   I shall endure,   for   not
endure   dreadful,   I shall suffer
                 wonderful

τοσοῦτον   οὐδὲν   ὥστε   μὴ   οὐ   καλῶς   θανεῖν.
tosouton   ouden   hōste   mē   ou   kalōs   thanein.
so great   nothing as   not   nobly   to die,
                                                   to be put to death,
                                                   to be dead

ΙΣ. ἀλλ'   εἰ δοκεῖ   σοι,   στεῖχε·   τοῦτο δ'   ἴσθ',   ὅτι
     all(a) ei dokei   soi,   steiche;   touto d(e) isth(i),   hoti
     well   if it seems to you   go,   this   but   know   that
                 best   depart

ἄνους   μὲν ἔρχῃ,   τοῖς   φίλοις   δ'   ὀρθῶς   φίλη.
anous   men erchēi,   tois   philois   d(e) orthōs philē.
witless,   you go   to (your) dear   truly   dear
without   (ones)
understanding   those loving you

endure this terror. I shall not suffer anything so evil as an
ignoble death.

     IS. Proceed if you must. But know this: despite your
folly, your loved ones truly love you.

THE PARODOS: A SUMMARY

The Chorus of Theban elders now dance onto the empty orchestra and celebrate their triumph over the Argive foe during the
past night. They address their song of joy and thanksgiving to
the rising sun. They sing of the haughty invader, Polynices,
leading the Seven against their city Thebes, and of the mutual
slaughter of the two brothers, Polynices and Eteocles. And
although they believe Polynices' death was a just reward for
his act of arrogance, their interest is joy and not blame as
Victory returns to Thebes. They call on Dionysos to lead them
in a night of revels. Thus, this choral song erases the con-
spiratorial tone of the Prologue and prepares for the majestic
entry of the new king.

The First Episode

THE SETTING

Creon's First Speech introduces the First Episode and gives the
audience its initial impression of the king. The playwright
thus adopts a paratactical structure, presenting each antago-
nist separately before they meet in heated confrontation in the
Second Episode (441 ff.).

After this initial address by the new king, the rest of the
First Episode concerns the guard's report of the so-called
"first burial" of Polynices. This humorous, garrulous country
bumpkin makes his report with evident terror. Creon's imme-
diate retort ("What man dared to do it?" 248) shows how unpre-
pared he will be for the guard's subsequent return with a
female culprit after the "second burial" (384 ff.). The king
reacts frenetically to the guard's news, accusing him of bribery and vowing to hang him alive if he does not find the rebel.
The scene achieves its power from the involvement of both Creon
and the guard in the action. The guard is not the usual
detached messenger but is the man responsible for preventing
the deed. The king's accusations strike a particularly
inappropriate note in the wake of the Chorus's suggestion that
the burial was god-inspired (theēlaton, 278). The audience,
surmising that Antigone performed the deed, knows how unjusti-
fied the charge of bribery is. And, if the burial is somehow
god-wrought, Creon's vow to Zeus to punish the culprit has a
peculiar irony.

The First Episode, then, shows a progression from the
Chorus's initial confidence in the new king to their final
misgivings. The following selection is the king's inaugural
address, spoken to his chosen, loyal elders, and their hesi-
tant reply (161-214). (See the introduction to "Creon's First
Speech," chap. 2 of the Guide, for a stylistic comparison to
Antigone's initial speech in the Prologue.)

CREON'S FIRST SPEECH AND THE REPLY OF THE CHORUS, 161-214

ΚΡΕΩΝ   CREON

ἄνδρες,	τὰ μὲν	δὴ	πόλεος	ἀσφαλῶς	θεοὶ
men, sirs	the affairs on the one hand, as for the affairs	indeed, at last	of the city, of the state	safely	gods

πολλῷ	σάλῳ	σείσαντες	ὤρθωσαν	πάλιν·
on much	surge, rolling swell	having tossed, disturbed	have made upright, straight, restored to health	set again to

ὑμᾶς	δ'	ἐγὼ	πομποῖσιν	ἐκ	πάντων	δίχα
you	but, on the other hand	I	by messengers	from	all	apart, in two, aloof

ἔστειλ'	ἱκέσθαι,	τοῦτο μὲν	τὰ Λαΐου	165
I gathered up, summoned	to come, to reach	this, in the first place	the of Laios	

σέβοντας	εἰδὼς	εὖ	θρόνων	ἀεὶ	κράτη,
loyal, revering	knowing well		of chair of state, of the throne	ever, always successive	powers

τοῦτ'	αὖθις,	ἡνίκ'·	Οἰδίπους	ὤρθου	πόλιν,
this secondly	again	at the time when	Oedipus	was keeping straight, ruling	the city

κἀπεὶ	διώλετ',	ἀμφὶ	τοὺς κείνων	ἔτι
and when he	perished	near, surrounding (i.e., in defense)	the of them (i.e., Oedipus' sons)	still

παῖδας	μένοντας	ἐμπέδοις	φρονήμασιν.
sons	standing firm, being true to	(with) firm, steadfast, unwavering	spirit, thoughts, purpose, will

ὅτ'	οὖν	ἐκεῖνοι	πρὸς	διπλῆς μοίρας	μίαν	170
when	therefore	those, they	by	double portion, doom	one	

καθ'   ἡμέραν   ὥλοντο   παίσαντές   τε   καὶ
on   day   perished having struck down   both and

πληγέντες   αὐτόχειρι   σὺν   μιάσματι,
having been   of kinsman's murder,   with stain, pollution,
smitten   suicidal,   violence
              fratricidal, murderous

ἐγὼ   κράτη   δὴ   πάντα   καὶ   θρόνους   ἔχω
I   powers now all   and   the throne I have, possess

γένους κατ'   ἀγχιστεῖα   τῶν   ὀλωλότων.
of   according to,   right of inheritance, of the deceased,
family on account of,   being nearest in kin   perished
       by privilege of

ἀμήχανον   δὲ   παντὸς ἀνδρὸς ἐκμαθεῖν   175
(it is) impossible now of any man   to know fully well

ψυχήν   τε   καὶ φρόνημα   καὶ γνώμην,   πρὶν ἂν
soul, nature both and spirit, way and judgment, until
                       of thinking   meaning

ἀρχαῖς   τε   καὶ νόμοισιν ἐντριβὴς   φανῇ.
administrative both and laws   (lit., rubbed), he appears
acts   engaged in,
                                    experienced in

    CR.   Sirs, the gods who tossed our city's bark on a
mighty surge have set it straight again. So now I have sum-
moned you to this meeting apart from all because I know you
always revered the power when Laios held the throne and again
when Oedipus guided the city's course, and after his death you
still stood by his sons with steadfast purpose. So since those
sons each perished by a double doom on one day, each striking
a kinsman and each smitten with a polluted hand, I now hold all
the powers of the throne by right of kinship with the deceased.
    One cannot fully know the nature, spirit, and judgment of
any man until he proves himself in administration of the laws.

ἐμοὶ   γὰρ   ὅστις   πᾶσαν   εὐθύνων   πόλιν
to me   for   whoever   the whole   guiding, governing   city

μὴ   τῶν   ἀρίστων   ἅπτεται   βουλευμάτων,
not   the   best   holds to, grasps,   plans, policy
                       cleaves to

ἀλλ'   ἐκ   φόβου   του   γλῶσσαν   ἐγκλήσας   ἔχει,   180
but   from   fear   some   tongue   locking up has
                               (i.e., has shut,
                               keeps shut)

κάκιστος   εἶναι   νῦν   τε   καὶ   πάλαι   δοκεῖ·
worst, most base   to be   now   both   and   of old   seems

καὶ μεῖζον·   ὅστις   ἀντὶ   τῆς αὑτοῦ πάτρας
and greater,   whoever   in comparison with,   his own   fatherland
   more   when set against
   important

φίλον   νομίζει,   τοῦτον   οὐδαμοῦ   λέγω.
relative,   considers,   him   as nothing   I hold
friend   recognizes

ἐγὼ γάρ,   ἴστω   Ζεὺς   ὁ   πάνθ'   ὁρῶν   ἀεί,
I   for   let know   Zeus   the one   all (things)   seeing   always

οὔτ'   ἂν   σιωπήσαιμι   τὴν   ἄτην   ὁρῶν   185
not   I would be silent   the   ruin   seeing

στείχουσαν   ἀστοῖς   ἀντὶ   τῆς   σωτηρίας,
advancing on,   townsmen,   in place of   the   welfare, safety,
menacing   citizens   prosperity

οὔτ'   ἂν   φίλον   ποτ'   ἄνδρα   δυσμενῆ   χθονὸς
nor   dear, friend   ever   man   hostile   to the land

θείμην   ἐμαυτῷ,   τοῦτο   γιγνώσκων   ὅτι
I would hold,   to myself   this   knowing, being   that
I would regard as   convinced

ἥδ'   ἐστὶν   ἡ   σῴζουσα   καὶ   ταύτης   ἔπι
she   is   the one   keeping safe, and   her   on
                             preserving

πλέοντες   ὀρθῆς   τοὺς   φίλους   ποιούμεθα.   190
sailing   straight the   friends we make, adopt

τοιοῖσδ'   ἐγὼ   νόμοισι   τήνδ'   αὔξω   πόλιν.
by such   I   principles, laws,   this   I intend to   city
as these   rules of conduct   make prosperous

καὶ   νῦν   ἀδελφὰ   τῶνδε   κηρύξας   ἔχω
and   now   akin   to these proclaiming I have
                                    I have proclaimed

ἀστοῖσι   παίδων   τῶν   ἀπ'   Οἰδίπου   πέρι·
to the townsmen, sons   the   of   Oedipus   concerning
to citizens

'Ετεοκλέα   μέν,   ὃς   πόλεως   ὑπερμαχῶν
Eteocles   who   city   fighting in behalf of

ὄλωλε   τῆσδε,   πάντ'   ἀριστεύσας   δορί, 195
perished this   all   having gained the prize for   with
                         valor, having shown all prowess spear

For I believe that whoever does not follow the best possible
policy in guiding the state but is tongue-tied from fear is
most base of men living or dead. And I utterly condemn the man
who puts the interests of a friend before those of his fatherland.

       Let all-seeing Zeus be my witness. For never would I be
silent when I see ruin menacing the city's welfare, and never
would I consider my country's foe as my friend. For I know
this: our country keeps us safe, and it is when we sail on her
even keel that we make friends. These are the principles by
which I intend to make the city prosperous. And now accord-
ingly I have published an edict to the townspeople concerning
the sons of Oedipus: Eteocles who died fighting for the city
after a valiant defense with his spear

τάφῳ   τε   κρύψαι   καὶ   τὰ   πάντ'   ἀφαγνίσαι
in tomb   both   to cover   and   all   to consecrate

ἃ   τοῖς   ἀρίστοις   ἔρχεται   κάτω   νεκροῖς·
which   to the bravest,   come, fall   below   corpses
                  noblest   to lot of

τὸν   δ'   αὖ   ξύναιμον   τοῦδε,   Πολυνείκη   λέγω,
the   but on the   brother   of him   Polynices   I mean
           other hand

ὃς   γῆν   πατρῷαν   καὶ   θεοὺς   τοὺς   ἐγγενεῖς
who   land of his fathers and   gods   the   of his race

φυγὰς   κατελθὼν   ἠθέλησε   μὲν   πυρὶ   200
runaway,   having come   wished   on the   with
fugitive   back from exile   one hand fire

πρῆσαι   κατάκρας,   ἠθέλησε   δ'   αἵματος
to fill full utterly, from   wished   on the   blood
of, consume   top to bottom   other hand

κοινοῦ   πάσασθαι,   τοὺς   δὲ   δουλώσας   ἄγειν,
common,   to feed on,   the rest   having   to lead
kindred   taste   enslaved

τοῦτον   πόλει   τῇδ'   ἐκκεκήρυκται   τάφῳ
this man   to city   this   it has been proclaimed   in tomb

μήτε   κτερίζειν   μήτε   κωκῦσαί   τινα,
neither   to bury with   nor   to lament   anyone
            funeral rites

ἐᾶν   δ'   ἄθαπτον   καὶ   πρὸς   οἰωνῶν   δέμας   205
to leave   but   unburied   both by   birds   body

καὶ   πρὸς   κυνῶν   ἐδεστὸν   αἰκισθέν   τ'   ἰδεῖν.
and   by   dogs   eaten   treated shamefully,   and to see,
                               outraged   to behold

τοιόνδ᾽	ἐμὸν	φρόνημα,	κοὔποτ᾽	ἔκ	γ᾽	ἐμοῦ
such	my	purpose, decision, thoughts	and never	from	at least by an act of mine	me at least

τιμῇ	προέξουσ᾽	οἱ	κακοὶ	τῶν	ἐνδίκων.
honor, worth	will hold more	the	evil (men)	than the, in preference to	righteous

ἀλλ᾽	ὅστις	εὔνους	τῇδε	τῇ	πόλει,	θανὼν
but	whoever	well-disposed	to this		city	dead

καὶ	ζῶν	ὁμοίως	ἐξ	ἐμοῦ	τιμήσεται.	210
and	living	in like manner, equally	from	me	he will be honored	

shall be interred with full funeral rites due to the most noble
dead; but his own brother--I mean Polynices--returned as fugitive, zealous to burn his fatherland and the temples of his
people from top to bottom, zealous to drink kindred blood and
to enslave the survivors. It is my proclamation to the city
that no one may bury this man with funeral rites nor mourn for
him; his body shall be left unburied to be mangled and outraged
by birds and dogs.

    This is my decision. Never shall I be one to hold the
evil in more esteem than the righteous. On the contrary, it is
my decision that the man who loves the city will be honored in
life and in death.

XO. σοὶ   ταῦτ'   ἀρέσκει,   παῖ Μενοικέως,   ποιεῖν
CHO. to you these (things) are pleasing son of Menoeceus to do

τὸν τῇδε   δύσνουν   καὶ τὸν εὐμενῆ   πόλει·
the to this ill-disposed, and the well-disposed, to the
              foe   friend   city

νόμῳ δὲ   χρῆσθαι παντί πού γ' ἔνεστί   σοι
law   but   to use   any,   I suppose it is in   to you
                     every   power

καὶ   τῶν θανόντων χὠπόσοι   ζῶμεν   πέρι.
both the dead   and whoever   we live concerning
                     of us

    CHO. Such is your pleasure, Creon, son of Menoeceus
toward the city's friend and foe. It is within your power, I
suppose, to legislate at will for the dead and those of us who
live.

3

The Ode on Man, 332-75

This famous ode occurs after Creon's ill-founded accusation of
bribery and after the Chorus's suggestion of divine complicity
in Polynices' burial. The actors then retreat and the Chorus
sings and dances the ode. (See the Introduction for the
androgynous dimension of the ode, and see the introduction to
the "Ode on Man," chap. 3 of the Guide, for a note on choral
rhythms.) The ode repeats the general progression of the
First Episode from initial confidence to final uncertainty.
The Chorus begins singing of mankind's glorious, daring
grandeur (see Guide, note on line 332 on deinos) and finally
retreats into a narrow condemnation of the very quality it
extolled. For a selective bibliography on this most famous of
all odes from classical drama, see the Guide.

Strophe A

πολλὰ	τὰ	δεινὰ	κούδὲν	ἀν-
polla	ta	deina	k(ai) ouden	an-
many	the	fearful, terrible, violent, alarming, strange, excessive, wonderful, awesome, marvelous, powerful, daring, skillful, clever, fierce, rigid	and nothing (yet)	

θρώπου	δεινότερον	πέλει
thrōpou	deinoteron	pelei;
(than) man	more strange, wondrous (etc.)	is wont, is

τοῦτο	καὶ	πολιοῦ	πέραν
touto	kai	poliou	perān
this		grey, clear, serene	to the further side of, across

πόντου	χειμερίῳ	νότῳ	335
pontou	cheimeriōi	notōi	
sea	wintry, raging	south wind	

χωρεῖ	περιβρυχίοισιν
chōrei	peribrychioisin
goes	engulfing

περῶν	ὑπ᾽	οἴδμασιν,	θεῶν
perōn	hyp(o)	oidmasin,	theōn
passing through	under	swells, waves, swollen waves	of the gods

τε	τὰν	ὑπερτάταν,	Γᾶν
te	tān	hypertatān,	Gān
and	the	supreme, eldest, highest, most exalted	Earth

ἄφθιτον,	ἀκαμάταν	ἀποτρύεται,
aphthiton,	akamatān	apotruetai,
imperishable, undecaying, unchanging, unchangeable	unwearied	rubs away, wears out

ἰλλομένων   ἀρότρων   ἔτος εἰς ἔτος,   340
illomenōn   arotrōn   etos eis etos,
turning around   plows   year by   year
(i.e., at furrow's end)

ἱππείῳ   γένει   πολεύων.
hippeiōi   genei   poleuōn.
of horses   offspring   going up and down,
                            turning up (soil)

Strophe A

Wonders are many, and nothing is more wondrously strange
than man. Impelled by the wintry wind, he crosses over the
grey sea, making his way through waves that threaten to engulf
him. He subdues that most exalted mother of the gods, Earth,
the imperishable and inexhaustible. His plows go back and
forth year after year as he tears up her soil with his mule.

Antistrophe A

κουφονόων   τε   φῦλον   ὀρ-
kouphonoōn   te   phȳlon   or-
nimble, flighty,   race
light-hearted

νίθων   ἀμφιβαλὼν   ἀγρεῖ
nīthōn   amphibalōn   agrei
of birds   ensnaring,   hunts
                 encompassing   after

καὶ   θηρῶν   ἀγρίων   ἔθνη
kai   thērōn   agriōn   ethnē
and   of beasts   living in the   tribes
                    fields, savage

πόντου   τ'   εἰναλίαν   φύσιν   345
pontou   t(e)   einaliān   physin
of the sea   and   of the sea,   species
                     marine

σπείραισι   δικτυοκλώστοις,
speiraisi   diktyoklōstois,
with twisted cords   woven into nets,
                         of woven nets

περιφραδὴς   ἀνήρ·   κρατεῖ
periphradēs   anēr;   kratei
very thoughtful, skillful,   man,   he masters, controls,
resourceful, clever,   male   gets the upper hand
universal-minded

δὲ   μαχαναῖς   ἀγραύλου
de   māchanais   agraulou
and   with contrivances,   having a dwelling in the open,
        skills   living in a wild lair

θηρὸς   ὀρεσσιβάτα   λασιαύχενά   θ'   350
thēros   oressibatā   lasiauchena   t(e)
beast   mountain-roaming with rough shaggy neck and

ἵππον	ὑπαξέμεν	ἀμφίλοφον	ζυγὸν
hippon	hypaxemen	amphilophon	zdygon
horse	lead under (yoke)	around the neck	yoke

οὔρειόν	τ'	ἀκμῆτα	ταῦρον.
oureion	t(e)	akmēta	tauron.
mountain	and	unwearied	bull

Antistrophe A

The tribe of blithe birds he hunts down and ensnares; the
tribes of wild beasts and the brood of the briny deep he
catches in his netted toils, the man of many skills. Again,
with his devices he masters the wild beast roaming the high-
land. He yokes the shaggy-necked steed and tames the tireless
mountain bull.

Strophe B

καὶ   φθέγμα   καὶ   ἀνεμόεν
kai   phthegma   kai   ānemoen
and   speech, language,   and   wind-swift,
       sound of voice   high-soaring

φρόνημα   καὶ   ἀστυνόμους   355
phronēma   kai   astynomous
thought   and   connected with governing
                    town-life, regulating cities

ὀργὰς   ἐδιδάξατο   καὶ   δυσαύλων
orgās   edidaxato   kai   dysaulōn
temper,   he has taught   and   of inhospitable
disposition himself

πάγων   ὑπαίθρεια   καὶ
pagōn   hypaithreia   kai
frosts   under the sky,   and
         in the open air

δύσομβρα   φεύγειν   βέλη
dysombra   pheugein   belē
tempestuous, (how) to flee   arrows, darts,
stormy   to avoid   shafts

παντοπόρος·   ἄπορος   ἐπ'   οὐδὲν   ἔρχεται   360
pantoporos;   aporos   ep(i)   ouden   erchetai
everywhere   pathless   to   nothing   he comes
journeying,   at a loss,
all-resourceful   resourceless

τὸ   μέλλον·   Ἅιδα   μόνον
to   mellon;   Haida   monon
the   future   Hades   only, alone

φεῦξιν   οὐκ   ἐπάξεται·
pheuxin   ouk   epaxetai;
a means of   not   he will procure for himself, devise for
escape   himself, bring to his aid, invent means

νόσων	δ'	ἀμαχάνων	φυγὰς
nosōn	d(e)	amāchanōn	phygās
from diseases		impossible, without remedy, beyond cure	flight, avoidance, means of escape

ξυμπέφρασται.

xympephrastai.

with others he has jointly devised

Strophe B

Language and thought swift as wind and the temper to live
in towns--all this he has taught himself; in finding shelter
from inhospitable frosts and sleet, man is all-resourceful. He
faces nothing in his future without resources. Against Hades
alone he can procure no escape. Yet, in concert with others,
he has learned to elude incurable diseases.

Antistrophe B

σοφόν	τι	τὸ	μαχανόεν	365
sophon	ti	to	māchanoen	
wise, cunning, shrewd	something	the	ingeniousness, inventive quality	

τέχνας	ὑπὲρ	ἐλπίδ᾽	ἔχων
technās	hyper	elpid(a)	echōn
of (his) skill, craft	beyond, exceeding	expectation, hope	having, possessing

τοτὲ	μὲν	κακόν,	ἄλλοτ᾽	ἐπ᾽	ἐσθλὸν	ἕρπει,
tote	men	kakon,	allot(e)	ep(i)	esthlon	herpei,
now, at one time		(to) evil	now, at another	to	moral goodness	inclines, moves

νόμους	παρείρων	χθονὸς
nomous	pareirōn	chthonos
laws	weaving into, into, when he weaves into	if he weaves into	of the earth, city, country

θεῶν	τ᾽	ἔνορκον	δίκαν,
theōn	t(e)	enorkon	dikān,
of the gods	and	bound by oath, that to which one has sworn	justice, order, right

ὑψίπολις·	ἄπολις	ὅτῳ	τὸ	μὴ	καλὸν	370
hypsipolis;	apolis	hotōi	to	mē	kalon	
high in the city, high in his city, he dwells in a proud city	cityless, banished from his city	for whom	the		not noble	

ξύνεστι	τόλμας	χάριν.
xynesti	tolmās	charin.
is with, is engaged in, dwells with, is associated with	daring, recklessness	for the sake of, on account of, thanks to

μήτ'   ἐμοὶ   παρέστιος
mēt(e)   emoi   parestios
not   to me   by the hearth,
                            sharer of the hearth

γένοιτο   μήτ'   ἴσον   φρονῶν
genoito   mēt(e)   ison   phronōn
let him be   and not   like (i.e., like-minded)   thinking

ὃς   τάδ'   ἔρδοι.
hos   tad(e)   erdoi.
who   these things does, should do

Antistrophe B

He possesses a shrewd inventive genius beyond expecta-
tion--yet he comes now to evil and now to good. But if he
weaves the laws of the land in with the justice of the gods to
whom oath binds him, he stands high in the city; banished from
the city is the one who rashly contaminates himself with sin.
May such a man never share my hearth or thoughts.

4

The Second Episode and

the Ode on *Atē*

As if in response to the Chorus's pietistic finale in the Ode on Man ("May the man who contaminates himself with sin never share my hearth or thoughts"), the bumptious guard reenters with the "transgressor," Antigone. Thus begins the Second Episode in which the confrontation between Antigone and Creon constitutes the centerpiece. Two three-cornered scenes frame this battle of the antagonists; in the first the guard occupies the third corner, in the other, Ismene.

In the first frame the guard with culprit in hand eagerly tells the tale of the capture. Creon hears only the incredible fact that Antigone sprinkled dust on the traitor's body in clear defiance of his command.[1] The audience hears other things: how the dust storm was somehow heaven-sent (421); how the girl had shrieked like a mother bird robbed of her nestling (423); how she endured her own violent capture with imperturbable composure, once she covered the body. The image of the mother bird protecting her young and becoming herself the hunted takes the audience back to the previous ode in which Mother Earth, and "light-hearted birds" each in turn endure man's domination (see Guide, notes on lines 337-38, 342). Yet, like Mother Earth, she appears at once both subjugated and indestructible ("Man subdues that most exalted mother of the gods, Earth, the imperishable and inexhaustible," 337-40).

In this first frame, then, the three uncommunicating char-

acters stand in marked contrast, each to the others, utterly
wrapped in his or her own concern. The guard, expressing some
compassion for the captured bird, is nevertheless primarily
filled with joyful relief at his own good fortune; the king is
overcome with disbelief at his niece's transgression of his
"law"; and Antigone has passed from piercing cry to
indestructible calm.

In the second frame, Ismene tries lovingly but unsuccess-
fully to implicate herself in her brother's burial. And when
Creon rashly damns the two sisters, calling them the "twin
vipers" he was nourishing in his house (531-32), her wish is
almost fulfilled. But Antigone cannot forgive Ismene's earlier
paralysis and coldly, even harshly, consigns her to continued
existence with Creon (549). Is this only apparent coldness on
Antigone's part, as some claim? Does she dissociate Ismene
from the burial in order to save her? Nothing in the text suggests such "charity." In fact, given Antigone's belief that
love constitutes life, and given Ismene's avowals of love,
Antigone must have known that Ismene's fate was worse than her
own. Ismene, too, would prefer physical death to death in
life.

These two scenes frame Antigone's encounter with the king in
which she gives eloquent but simple voice to her deep conviction that her act conformed to the only real law, the unwritten and unchanging law of Zeus. Her speech (the selection
below) wins no converts: the Chorus concludes that she is
obstinate (ōmos) like her father (471-72); Creon, that she has
overstepped "the established law" and, like a fiery horse,
needs a bridle. He has not comprehended her distinction
between his "decree" and genuine law (see the introduction to
"Defense of the Unwritten Laws, chap. 4 of the Guide, for the
different understandings of law in the play and in Greek
thought). Instead, Creon is preoccupied with the fear that she
is the man and not he, "if she flouts authority with impunity"
(484-85). Such is the setting and response to the following
speech (450-70) of Antigone, her "Defense of the Unwritten
Laws."

DEFENSE OF THE UNWRITTEN LAWS, 450-70

AN. οὐ γάρ τί   μοι   Ζεὺς ἦν   ὁ   κηρύξας   τάδε,   450
    not for in any   to me Zeus was the   proclaiming   these
          way   one   (things)

    οὐδ᾽   ἡ   ξύνοικος   τῶν   κάτω θεῶν Δίκη
    and not   the   dwelling   the   below gods Justice
                    together with

    τοιούσδ᾽   ἐν   ἀνθρώποισιν ὥρισεν   νόμους,
    such, of   among men,   defined, marked   laws
    such a kind   mankind   out, established

    οὐδὲ   σθένειν   τοσοῦτον   ᾠόμην   τὰ   σὰ
    nor   to be strong   so much   I did   the   your
              (i.e., had such weight)   think

    κηρύγμαθ᾽   ὥστ᾽   ἄγραπτα   κἀσφαλῆ   θεῶν
    proclamations   so that   unwritten   and unfailing, of the
                                            steadfast   gods

    νόμιμα   δύνασθαι   θνητὸν ὄνθ᾽ ὑπερδραμεῖν.   455
    customs, to be able mortal being to outrun, override,
    laws   transgress, prove
                                       stronger than

    οὐ γάρ τι   νῦν γε   κἀχθές,   ἀλλ᾽ ἀεί   ποτε
    not for something   now even and   but   always   ever
                                   yesterday   forever without end

    ζῇ   ταῦτα,   κοὐδεὶς οἶδεν ἐξ   ὅτου   ᾽φάνη.
    live, are   these   and no   knows from what (time),   they
    in force   one   (place)   appeared

    τούτων   ἐγὼ οὐκ ἔμελλον,   ἀνδρὸς   οὐδενὸς
    of these I   not was intending, was   of (a mere) (not) one,
                      about to, meant to   man   any

    φρόνημα δείσασ᾽,   ἐν   θεοῖσι τὴν δίκην
    will,   (I) fearing   in the tribunal gods   the penalty
    purpose   of, among the

δώσειν·	θανουμένη	γὰρ	ἐξῄδη,		τί	δ'	οὔ;	460
to pay	that I would be dying	for	I knew well		why	and	not	

κεἰ	μὴ	σὺ	προυκήρυξας.		εἰ δὲ	τοῦ	χρόνου
even if	not	you	had brought it publicly to my knowledge, proclaimed		if but	the (my)	time

πρόσθεν	θανοῦμαι,	κέρδος		αὔτ'	ἐγὼ	λέγω.
before	I shall die	gain, profit		this	I	declare

ὅστις	γὰρ	ἐν	πολλοῖσιν	ὡς	ἐγὼ	κακοῖς
whoever	for	among	many	as	I	evils

ζῇ,	πῶς	ὅδ'	οὐχὶ	κατθανὼν	κέρδος	φέρει;
lives	how	this person	not	dying	gain, profit	consider, bear

AN. In my belief, it was not Zeus who proclaimed this edict, and Justice who dwells with the gods below did not establish such "laws" among men, and I did not judge that your decrees had such strength that a mere mortal was able to override the unwritten and unfailing laws of the gods. For these laws are not a thing of today or yesterday, but they live forever and ever, and no one knows their origin. I was not about to pay the penalty for such disobedience in the divine court out of fear of any man's willful decision. For I knew well that I would die—how escape it?—even if you had not made your proclamation. And if I die before my time, I call it gain. For when one lives beset by evils, as I do, does not death bring gain?

οὕτως   ἔμοιγε   τοῦδε   τοῦ μόρου   τυχεῖν   465
thus, this   for me   this,   fate   to meet
being the case indeed   my

παρ' οὐδὲν ἄλγος· ἀλλ' ἄν, εἰ τὸν ἐξ ἐμῆς
of no account pain   but   if the of my own

μητρὸς θανόντ'   ἄθαπτον   ἠνσχόμην   νέκυν,
mother (when) dead unburied I had allowed (to be)   corpse

κείνοις ἄν ἤλγουν·   τοῖσδε   δ'   οὐκ ἀλγύνομαι.
at that   I would be   at this   but not do I grieve,
             grieving,   I am grieved
             feel pain

σοὶ   δ' εἰ δοκῶ νῦν μῶρα   δρῶσα τυγχάνειν,
to you but if I seem now foolish playing to happen
                             (part)

σχεδόν   τι μώρῳ μωρίαν ὀφλισκάνω.   470
all but   from a folly I am charged, stand
(perhaps)   fool   convicted, bear the charge

Thus, I feel no grief in facing this fate. But if I had left
my mother's dead son an unburied corpse, that would have
grieved me--I feel no grief at this. You think I behave fool-
ishly now? Perhaps it is a fool who convicts me of folly.

THE ODE ON ATĒ: A SUMMARY AND COMMENT

The ode (582-620) begins somberly: "Happy are those whose
lives have not tasted evil. For atē never leaves those whose
house has been shaken by the gods." The Chorus then proceeds
to muse on the inherited curse that continues to strike each
generation of the house of Laios. Now the final light of the
house is cut down (presumably in the person of Antigone). In
the second strophe, the Chorus widens its canvas: it sings of
the power of Zeus (604 ff.) in language and in Aeolic rhythms
that parallel those reserved for humanity in the Ode on Man.
The splendor of Zeus is contrasted with the unfailing law for
mortals: "Nothing excessive comes into human life without atē,
disaster" (613-14). The final antistrophe meditates on human
hopes, the deceptions of frivolous human desires, but it also
avows that no atē comes to one who is aware (618). The Chorus
ends on a despairing note: evil appears as good to the one whom
the god leads to infatuation (atē); for such a one, disaster
(atē) comes quickly. The ode's somber beginning and ending
surround the dazzling, happy description of the glory of Zeus.

One can see the poet bringing together much of Greek religious insight in this meditation on atē, a word with a long
history from its Homeric usage as an external force accounting
for man's irrational behavior, to the disaster Zeus imposed on
humanity, to the guilt men felt when conscious of sin, to
deliberate deception that leads victims to new errors and new
sins.[2]

This ode, like the previous one on humanity, is a generalizing song in which the Chorus steps aside from the action and
in ambiguous lyrical language considers the deeper problems
suggested by the action of the episodes. As with the earlier
ode, the application of this ode to the action is both ambiguous and ironical. The occasion for the ode is the disaster
that has struck Antigone, the last root of the house of Labdakos (599-600). The Chorus is convinced that she is suffering from the illusion that her act conforms to the divine
will. Yet the action of the play will show the false concep-

tion was primarily Creon's. It is his good counsel that
proves to be an illusion. His confident identification of his
own will with Zeus', his complete faith in the evidence of the
senses, his disregard for the law of a realm that transcends
that of the polis, his unquestioning belief that his decree is
in the state's best interest--all this brands him as the "man
whom the god will ruin."

Yet what is the poet's view in all of this? Clearly, he
does not share the Chorus's view that the curse of the house of
Labdakos falls on Antigone rather than on Creon. Is, then, the
curse nothing supernatural in Sophocles' view but rather "a
repetition of human evil by a man [i.e., by Creon] too foolish
to mark the warnings of family history"?[3] This view takes too
little notice of the supernatural elements so persistently
present in the play and the ode. Does the poet share his
Chorus's view that destructive atē does not strike one who is
aware (618)? Hardly, since Antigone's piety and awareness do
not save her from destruction.

There is much that is both profound about this ode and
impenetrable as one tries to understand the relation between
the words of the Chorus here and the poet's vision of reality.
One is struck by the darkening of the atmosphere and vision
from the earlier ode on man: there splendor, light, and
victory were associated with human powers; here humanity is
lost in the sea of disaster, and only Zeus is splendid and
unaging, as destructive atē seems to destroy indiscriminately
both the one who is aware and the deluded fool.[4]   This dark
song, then, is the prelude to the Third Episode in which the
king's dutiful son Haemon attempts to save his father from atē
through the light of reason.

5

The Third Episode and

the Ode on Eros

THE SETTING

As the Chorus completes the Ode on Atē, it sees Creon's young son, Haemon, approaching and wonders whether he is "highly disturbed" out of sympathy for his fiancée, Antigone (627-30). But the deferential tone of his opening words allays his father's fears.

The selection provided below (631-765) constitutes almost the entire Third Episode (631-780). In the debate, the young man limits himself to the weapons of reason and filial piety. Only in his final anger (762-66) does the audience see the passion he so carefully represses until that point. Thus, Haemon's departure signals the complete rupture of his respect for his father. However, after he stamps off, his father makes a concession quite appropriate to his legalistic view of piety: Antigone need not die. Instead, she will be buried alive, entombed with enough food so that the city may avoid miasma (773-76). Let her call on Hades, the only god whom she reveres (777-90), the king concludes. Such is the king's response to his son's arguments and anger.

(See the Introduction for evidence of Haemon's "gynecandrous" character; see the introduction to the "Creon-Haemon Debate," chap. 5 in the Guide, for a discussion of the themes of emptiness, piety, and obedience in this episode.)

THE CREON-HAEMON DEBATE, 631-765

KP. τάχ'   εἰσόμεσθα   μάντεων   ὑπέρτερον.
    quickly   we shall know   (than) seers   more surely

ὦ παῖ,   τελείαν   ψῆφον   ἄρα   μὴ   κλύων
O son   final,   pebble,   surely not hearing
           authoritative   vote, decree

τῆς   μελλονύμφου   πατρὶ   λυσσαίνων   πάρει;
of the betrothed   father   raving against   have you come here

ἦ   σοὶ   μὲν   ἡμεῖς   πανταχῇ   δρῶντες   φίλοι;
or   to you at least we   everywhere, in   acting   friends,
                               every respect   dear

ΑΙΜΩΝ   HAEMON

πάτερ,   σός   εἰμι·   καὶ   σύ   μοι   γνώμας   ἔχων   635
father   yours I am   and   you   to me,   counsels having
                                       for me

χρηστὰς   ἀπορθοῖς,   αἷς   ἔγωγ'   ἐφέψομαι,
good,   you make   which   I   I shall
favorable,   straight,   follow,
serviceable   straighten   pursue

ἐμοὶ   γὰρ   οὐδεὶς   ἀξιώσεται   γάμος
to me   for   no   will be valued, esteemed   marriage

μείζων   φέρεσθαι   σοῦ   καλῶς   ἡγουμένου.
greater, better   to win   you   well   guiding
                                           if, when, you guide well

KP. οὕτω   γάρ,   ὦ   παῖ,   χρὴ   διὰ   στέρνων   ἔχειν,
    thus   yes   O   son   it is   in   breast,   to be
                                    necessary   heart   disposed

γνώμης   πατρῴας   πάντ'   ὄπισθεν   ἐστάναι.   640
judgment   (your)   in all   behind   to stand
              father's   (things)

τούτου   γὰρ   οὕνεκ'   ἄνδρες   εὔχονται   γονὰς
this   on account of   men   pray   offspring

κατηκόους   φύσαντες   ἐν   δόμοις   ἔχειν,
listening, obedient   having begotten   in   homes   to have

ὡς   καὶ   τὸν ἐχθρὸν   ἀνταμύνωνται   κακοῖς,
so that both   the foe, hated one   they may requite,   with evil
                                   reward

καὶ   τὸν   φίλον   τιμῶσιν   ἐξ ἴσου   πατρί.
and   the   friend   they may honor equally   as the father

ὅστις   δ'   ἀνωφέλητα   φιτύει   τέκνα,   645
whoever   but   unprofitable, worthless   sows, begets children

τί   τόνδ'   ἂν   εἴποις   ἄλλο   πλὴν   αὐτῷ   πόνους
what   this   would you say   else,   except   for   troubles
        one   other   himself

CR. We will soon know better than a seer could know.
Son, you have heard my final decision about your fiancée.
Surely you are not here to rave against your father on her
behalf, are you? Or am I dear to you at least no matter how I
act?

HAE. Father, I am yours. And when you guide well, you
set a straight path for me, and I for one shall follow it. For
I shall esteem no marriage more highly than your guidance, when
it is wise.

CR. Yes, son, this ought to be your heart's instinct, to
give the front rank to your father's judgment in all matters.
This is what men pray for, to beget and possess obedient offspring in their homes, children who will repay their father's
foes with evil and who will honor his friends even as the
father does. But if he begets unprofitable children, what
would you say he has fathered but trouble for himself

φῦσαι,   πολὺν   δὲ   τοῖσιν   ἐχθροῖσιν   γέλων;
to have   much   but for the enemies   occasion
begotten   for laughter

μὴ   νύν   ποτ᾽,   ὦ παῖ,   τὰς φρένας γ᾽ ὑφ᾽   ἡδονῆς
do not then ever   O son   reason   under   pleasure
                                                influence of

γυναικὸς   οὕνεκ᾽   ἐκβάλῃς,   εἰδὼς   ὅτι
woman   for the sake of overthrow, cast away knowing that

ψυχρὸν   παραγκάλισμα   τοῦτο   γίγνεται, 650
chill, cold, thing to clasp,   this (i.e., the   becomes
joyless   embrace, comfort   following thing)

γυνὴ   κακὴ   ξύνευνος   ἐν   δόμοις. τί   γὰρ
woman, wife evil   bedfellow, spouse in   home   what   for

γένοιτ᾽   ἂν   ἕλκος   μεῖζον   ἢ   φίλος   κακός;
would be   ulcer, wound greater than   friend   bad

ἀλλὰ   πτύσας   ὡσεί   τε   δυσμενῆ   μέθες
on the   spitting out,   like, as if (being) enemy set loose,
contrary   spurning   dismiss

τὴν   παῖδ᾽ ἐν   Ἅιδου   τήνδε νυμφεύειν τινί.
the   girl   in   (the house of) Hades this   to marry   someone

ἐπεὶ   γὰρ   αὐτὴν   εἷλον   ἐμφανῶς   ἐγὼ   655
since   for   her   I have seized   openly   I

πόλεως   ἀπιστήσασαν   ἐκ   πάσης   μόνην,
city   disobeying   from   all   alone

ψευδῆ   γ᾽   ἐμαυτὸν   οὐ   καταστήσω   πόλει,
false   indeed myself   not   I will render   to the city

ἀλλὰ   κτενῶ.   πρὸς ταῦτ᾽ ἐφυμνείτω   Δία
but   I shall kill therefore   let her invoke repeatedly Zeus

ξύναιμον·   εἰ γὰρ δὴ   τά γ᾽ ἐγγενῆ   φύσει
of common blood,   if for indeed the   kindred   by birth
presiding over kindred

ἄκοσμα   θρέψω,   κάρτα   τοὺς ἔξω   γένους.   660
disorderly, I am to   all the   those outside of race,
unruly   nourish   more   family

ἐν   τοῖς γὰρ οἰκείοισιν ὅστις   ἔστ᾽ ἀνὴρ
in the case of the   for household   whoever is   man

χρηστός,   φανεῖται   κἄν   πόλει δίκαιος ὤν.
good, upright, will appear also in city   just   being
serviceable

ὅστις   δ᾽ ὑπερβὰς   ἢ   νόμους βιάζεται,   663
whoever but overstepping, either laws   does
             transgressing   violence to

ἢ   τοὐπιτάσσειν   τοῖς κρατύνουσιν   νοεῖ,
or   to impose commands on those governing   thinks

and much laughter for his enemies? Then, son, whatever you do,
do not banish reason out of desire for a woman. You know that
an evil wife sharing your bed becomes a chilling embrace. For
what deeper ulcer can there be than an evil friend? No, loathe
this girl, cast her out as a foe for someone to marry in the
house of Hades. For since I have taken her alone of all the
city in open disobedience, I will not make myself a liar before
the city. No, I shall kill her. So let her keep praying to
Zeus, the god of kindred blood. For if I rear insubordination
in my very relatives, how much more will I rear it in out-
siders. Only a man who is praiseworthy in his own household
will be found just in the city also. But whoever transgresses
and violates the laws or presumes to impose commands on his
rulers

οὐκ ἔστ'   ἐπαίνου τοῦτον   ἐξ   ἐμοῦ τυχεῖν.   665
not is possible praise   this one from me   to attain

ἀλλ'   ὃν   πόλις   στήσειε,   τοῦδε χρὴ   κλύειν
but, no whom the city may appoint him   it is   to obey
                                         necessary

καὶ   σμικρὰ   καὶ   δίκαια   καὶ   τἀναντία.
both   in little   and   just (things) and   their
           (things)   opposites

καὶ   τοῦτον   ἂν   τὸν ἄνδρα   θαρσοίην   ἐγὼ   668
and   this one   man   I would believe   I
                                   confidently

καλῶς μὲν ἄρχειν,   εὖ   δ' ἂν ἄρχεσθαι   θέλειν,
well   to govern well and   to be governed to consent

δορός   τ' ἂν ἐν χειμῶνι   προστεταγμένον   670
spear, war and   in winter, storm stationed

μένειν   δίκαιον   κἀγαθὸν   παραστάτην.
to remain   just   and brave   comrade on the flank, one
                                    who stands by in battle

ἀναρχίας   δὲ   μεῖζον   οὐκ ἔστιν κακόν.   672
(than) lack of a leader, but greater no   is   evil
lawlessness, anarchy

αὕτη   πόλεις   τ'   ὄλλυσιν,   ἥδ'   ἀναστάτους
this   cities   both destroys   this   ruined, laid waste

οἴκους   τίθησιν·   ἥδε   τ'   ἐν μάχη   δορὸς
homes   makes   this and in battle   of spear, of
                                             military force

τροπὰς   καταρρήγνυσι·   τῶν   δ'   ὀρθουμένων   675
turnings,   causes to break   of   but going straight,
routs   forth, puts   those   being guided aright,
            into confusion   restored to health

σῴζει   τὰ πολλὰ σώμαθ᾿   ἡ πειθαρχία.

brings to safety   the many bodies, lives, persons   obedience

οὕτως   ἀμυντέ᾿ ἐστὶ   τοῖς κοσμουμένοις,

this being   it must be   the   orderly institutions, public
the case   defended   order, regulations

κοὔτοι   γυναικὸς   οὐδαμῶς   ἡσσητέα.

and   by a woman   in any way   one must be
indeed not   worsted, beaten

κρεῖσσον γάρ,   εἴπερ δεῖ,   πρὸς ἀνδρὸς ἐκπεσεῖν,

better   for   if   it is   by   a man   to be cut down,
                        necessary   banished, wrecked

κοὔκ   ἂν γυναικῶν   ἥσσονες   καλοίμεθ᾿   ἄν.   680

and not   (than) women inferior,   we should
             weaker   be called

KO. ἡμῖν   μέν,   εἰ μὴ   τῷ χρόνῳ   κεκλέμμεθα,

to us   indeed if, not   (by) age   we have been robbed,
                unless   are deceived

λέγειν   φρονούντως ὧν   λέγεις   δοκεῖς πέρι.

to say   wisely   (the things) you say   you   concerning
                      which   seem

cannot win praise from me. No! One must obey anyone the city
may appoint, both in small matters and in just, and in their
opposites. And I would confidently believe that an obedient
man will govern well and will be a good subject and that, when
stationed in a storm of spears, he will remain at his post, a
just, brave comrade. Anarchy is an evil without equal. This
destroys cities, this leaves homes desolate, this causes routs
on the battlefield. But obedience saves men's lives when their
course is upright. Therefore public decrees must be supported
and never must one be beaten by a woman in any way. For if one
must be displaced, better to be dethroned by a man. Never let
me be inferior to a woman.

     CHO. You seem to speak wisely, I think, unless our years
deceive us.

AI. πάτερ,   θεοὶ   φύουσιν   ἀνθρώποις   φρένας,
    father   gods   sow, implant   in men   reason, wisdom, sense

πάντων   ὅσ᾽   ἐστὶ   χρημάτων   ὑπέρτατον.
of all   as many as   are   possessions, blessings   the highest

ἐγὼ   δ᾽   ὅπως   σὺ   μὴ   λέγεις   ὀρθῶς   τάδε,   685
I   in what   you   not   say   rightly   these
             respect   (things)

οὔτ᾽   ἂν   δυναίμην   μήτ᾽   ἐπισταίμην   λέγειν·
not   I should   and may not   I may be   to say
               be able   capable of

γένοιτο   μέντἂν   χἀτέρως   καλῶς,   ἔχον.
might occur   however   also elsewhere,   well,   having
                            otherwise   something good

σὺ   δ᾽   οὐ   πέφυκας   πάντα   προσκοπεῖν   ὅσα
you   but   not   are in position   all   to observe   whatever

λέγει   τις   ἢ   πράσσει   τις   ἢ   ψέγειν   ἔχει.
says   anyone or   does   anyone   or   to blame   has

τὸ   γὰρ   σὸν   ὄμμα   δεινὸν   ἀνδρὶ   δημότῃ   690
      for   your   eye,   dread,   to a man,   private,
                      sight   terrifying   a citizen   common

. . . .
λόγοις   τοιούτοις,   οἷς   σὺ   μὴ   τέρψῃ   κλύων·
(from) words,   such   as   you   not   would be   hearing
(on account of)   pleased, enjoy

ἐμοὶ   δ᾽   ἀκούειν   ἔσθ᾽   ὑπὸ   σκότου   τάδε,
for me,   but   to hear   it is   in   the darkness,   these
to me   possible   the dark   (things)

τὴν   παῖδα   ταύτην   οἷ   ὀδύρεται   πόλις,
       girl   this   what, how   mourns   city

πασῶν   γυναικῶν   ὡς   ἀναξιωτάτη
of all   women   (saying) that   most undeserving

κάκιστ'	ἀπ'	ἔργων	εὐκλεεστάτων	φθίνει˙	695
most evilly, miserably	after, because of, in consequence of	deeds	most glorious, noble	she wastes away, dies	

ἥτις	τὸν	αὐτῆς	αὐτάδελφον	ἐν		φοναῖς
(since) she	the	of her own	very own brother	in the midst of		slaughter

πεπτῶτ'	ἄθαπτον	μήθ'	ὑπ'	ὠμηστῶν		κυνῶν
having fallen	unburied	neither	by	feeding on raw flesh, flesh-tearing		dogs

εἴασ'		ὀλέσθαι	μήθ'	ὑπ'	οἰωνῶν	τινός˙
would she allow, she did allow		to perish	nor	by	of birds	any

οὐχ	ἥδε	χρυσῆς	ἀξία	τιμῆς	λαχεῖν;
not	such a one as this, she	golden, noble, glorious	worthy	of honor	to obtain by lot, have assigned to one

τοιάδ'	ἐρεμνὴ	σῖγ'	ὑπέρχεται	φάτις.	700
of such a kind	black, dark	secretly	creeps upon, steals over	voice, rumor	

HAE. Father, the gods implant wisdom in mankind, the highest of all possessions. I would not be able--and may I never bring myself to say how you are wrong. Still perhaps some good thought may also come from another source. You are not in a position to observe all that men say or do or find fault with. And your expression is forbidding to the citizenry. . . when such words are spoken as would offend you. But I can hear words spoken in the darkness, how the city mourns for this girl. People are saying: "She of all women least deserves to die so shamefully for such noble deeds. Her very own brother died in bloody contest and she would not leave him an unburied prey for flesh-eating dogs and vultures. Does she not deserve the reward of golden honor?" Dark talk like this is quietly circulating.

ἐμοὶ   δὲ   σοῦ   πράσσοντος   εὐτυχῶς,   πάτερ,
for me   but   (than) faring   with good fortune,   father
                your   successfully

οὐκ   ἔστιν   οὐδὲν   κτῆμα   τιμιώτερον.
not   there is   no   possession,   more valued,
                              treasure   prized

τί   γὰρ   πατρὸς   θάλλοντος   εὐκλείας   τέκνοις
what   for   father   prospering (than) good   to children,
                                   repute, glory   for children

ἄγαλμα   μεῖζον,   ἢ   τί   πρὸς   παίδων   πατρί;
delight,   greater   or what   on the   the children for a father
ornament   part of

μὴ νυν ἓν ἦθος   μοῦνον ἐν σαυτῷ   φόρει,   705
not then one customary outlook,   alone in yourself wear,
             disposition,   bear,
             character   possess

ὡς   φὴς   σύ,   κοὐδὲν ἄλλο, τοῦτ' ὀρθῶς ἔχειν.
how   you speak   you   and   else this right is
(i.e., your way of speaking)   nothing

ὅστις   γὰρ αὐτὸς   ἢ   φρονεῖν   μόνος δοκεῖ,
whoever for himself either to have understanding, alone, thinks
                            to be wise

ἢ   γλῶσσαν,   ἣν   οὐκ ἄλλος,   ἢ   ψυχὴν   ἔχειν,
or tongue   which not another or soul, reason, mind, to have
   speech   understanding

οὗτοι   διαπτυχθέντες   ὤφθησαν   κενοί.
these (men) being unfolded, spread   appear   empty
(i.e., when one looks at them)

ἀλλ' ἄνδρα, κεἴ   τις ᾖ σοφός, τὸ μανθάνειν   710
but man   even though one be wise   to learn, learning

πόλλ'   αἰσχρὸν   οὐδὲν   καὶ τὸ μὴ τείνειν   ἄγαν.
many   disgraceful nothing and   not to strain   too much
(things)   (string)   (overtight)

ὁρᾷς	παρὰ	ῥείθροισι	χειμάρροις		ὅσα
you see	alongside	rivers, streams	swollen by storms		whatever

δένδρων	ὑπείκει,		κλῶνας	ὡς	ἐκσῴζεται,
of trees	yield, give away		twigs		that preserve (for oneself)

τὰ	δ'	ἀντιτείνοντ'	αὐτόπρεμν'	ἀπόλλυται.
those	but	stretching back, resisting	together with the roots	are destroyed

αὕτως	δὲ	ναὸς	ὅστις	ἐγκρατῆ		πόδα	715
even so	and	of a ship	whoever	with a firm hold, controlling		sheet	

τείνας	ὑπείκει	μηδέν,		ὑπτίοις	κάτω
stretching, holding taut	slackens	not at all		turned upside down	downward

στρέψας		τὸ	λοιπὸν	σέλμασιν	ναυτίλλεται.
upsetting (its)		the	rest	rowing benches	proceeds on the voyage

But I, Father, have no more precious possession than your good fortune. For what greater glory do children have than their father's good name, and what greater glory does a father have than his sons'? Please then, do not cling to only one outlook as if your word, and nothing else, is right. For whenever a man thinks that he alone is wise, or that he alone-- and no one else--has a tongue or has integrity, then when he is opened to public scrutiny, he proves to be empty. No, it is no disgrace even for a wise man to learn many things and not to be overtaut. In swollen rivers, you see that the trees that give way are the ones that save their branches and that the unbending ones perish, roots and all. Similarly,the mariner who holds the ship's sheet taut without slackening it at all capsizes and ends his voyage with benches upside down.

ἀλλ'   εἶκε,   θυμῷ   καὶ   μετάστασιν   δίδου.
no   yield   (to) wrath and   a change   allow, grant

γνώμη   γὰρ   εἰ   τις   κἀπ'   ἐμοῦ   νεωτέρου
sound   for   if   any   also from,   me   younger
opinion   even from

πρόσεστι,   φήμ'   ἔγωγε   πρεσβεύειν   πολὺ   720
is added,   I say I indeed to hold the first place, by far
contributed   be the best thing

φῦναί   τιν'   ἄνδρα   πάντ'   ἐπιστήμης   πλέων·
to be by a   man   altogether,   of knowledge full
nature   in all things

εἰ   δ'   οὖν,   φιλεῖ   γὰρ   τοῦτο   μὴ ταύτῃ   ῥέπειν,
if   but so   is   for   this   in not   to tilt,
     (not)   accustomed   this way   incline

καὶ   τῶν   λεγόντων   εὖ   καλὸν   τὸ   μανθάνειν.
also (from) those speaking   well   good   to learn, learning

XO. ἄναξ,   σέ   τ'   εἰκός,   εἴ τι   καίριον   λέγει,
    king   you both like the truth, if anything timely   he
                      reasonable   speaks

μαθεῖν,   σέ   τ'   αὖ   τοῦδ'· εὖ   γὰρ εἴρηται   διπλῇ.   725
to learn   you and in   from   well for it has been on both
from him   turn him   spoken   sides

KP. οἱ   τηλικοίδε   καὶ   διδαξόμεσθα   δὴ
    those   of such   even shall we go   now (at this late age)
    (of us) an age   to school

φρονεῖν   πρὸς ἀνδρὸς τηλικοῦδε   τὴν   φύσιν;
to learn (wisdom)   from a man of such an age (in) birth, age

AI. μηδὲν   τὸ   μὴ   δίκαιον·   εἰ   δ'   ἐγὼ   νέος,
    in nothing the   not just   if   but I   young
                     (i.e., that is not just)

οὐ τὸν χρόνον   χρὴ   μᾶλλον ἢ   τἄργα   σκοπεῖν.
not the (my) time, it is   rather than the (my)   to look
     years   necessary   deeds, the
                                          facts of
                                          the case

P. ἔργον   γάρ   ἐστι   τοὺς   ἀκοσμοῦντας   σέβειν;   730
   a deed   then   is it   the   being disorderly to pay
                                  (ones), mutinous   respect,
                                  offenders   to honor

I. οὐδ᾽   ἂν   κελεύσαιμ᾽   εὐσεβεῖν   ἐς   τοὺς   κακούς.
   not   would I   to honor,   for   the   wicked,
                urge, bid   respect   evildoers

P. οὐχ   ἥδε   γὰρ   τοιᾷδ᾽   ἐπείληπται   νόσῳ;
   not   she   then   with this   has been   disease,
                      kind of   seized   sickness

I. οὔ   φησι   Θήβης   τῆσδ᾽   ὁμόπτολις   λεώς.
   no   says   of Thebes this   from the same city   people
                                 (i.e., united, whole city)

        Do yield! Let your anger abate! For if my youth has any
wisdom, I declare it is best of all for a man to be naturally
endowed with the full knowledge. But if he is not--and this
is the more usual tilt of the scale--then it is honorable to
learn from those who speak wisely.
        CHO. King, it is reasonable for you to learn from him
when his words are apropos, and you, Haemon, from him. You
both have spoken reasonably.
        CR. Shall we at our age even now be schooled in wisdom
from a youngster like this?
        HAE. Not to learn anything unjust. I am young. But
study the facts of the case not my youth.
        CR. Is reverence to traitors one of your "facts"?
        HAE. I would not urge reverence for criminals.
        CR. Well, then, was not the girl inflicted with this
disease?
        HAE. "Not so," declares the united people of the city.

KP. πόλις γὰρ ἡμῖν ἁμὲ χρὴ τάσσειν ἐρεῖ;
city then, what! to us how me it is necessary to order, to rule will tell

AI. ὁρᾷς τόδ' ὡς εἴρηκας ὡς ἄγαν νέος; 735
do you see this that you have spoken like, as too, very young (i.e., childish)

KP. ἄλλῳ γὰρ ἢ 'μοὶ χρή με τῆσδ' ἄρχειν χθονός;
in another's interest then than in my interest ought, it is necessary me this to rule earth, land

AI. πόλις γὰρ οὐκ ἔσθ' ἥτις ἀνδρός ἐσθ' ἑνός.
city yes, for no is which (possession) of man is one

KP. οὐ τοῦ κρατοῦντος ἡ πόλις νομίζεται;
not (possession) of the one ruling, the master the city is considered, acknowledged

AI. καλῶς ἐρήμης γ' ἂν σὺ γῆς ἄρχοις μόνος.
well of desolate, empty you land would rule alone

KP. ὅδ', ὡς ἔοικε, τῇ γυναικὶ συμμαχεῖ. 740
this (man) as it seems (with) the woman is in league with, fights on the side of

AI. εἴπερ γυνὴ σύ· σοῦ γὰρ οὖν προκήδομαι.
if woman you you for assuredly I care for, I take thought for

KP. ὦ παγκάκιστε, διὰ δίκης ἰὼν πατρί.
O shameless one, utterly vile in controversy with, to law with engaging, going father

AI. οὐ γὰρ δίκαιά σ' ἐξαμαρτάνονθ' ὁρῶ.
no for just (things) justice you committing a fault against, offending against I see

KP. ἁμαρτάνω γὰρ τὰς ἐμὰς ἀρχὰς σέβων;
do I offend then the my own kingly powers, prerogatives respecting

Ι. οὐ γὰρ σέβεις, τιμάς   γε τὰς θεῶν πατῶν. 745
   not for you honors, at the of walking on,
         respect prerogatives any the tramping
                rate gods underfoot

Η. ὦ μιαρὸν   ἦθος   καὶ γυναικὸς ὕστερον.
   O bloodstained, disposition, and a woman coming after,
      foul character inferior to

Ι. οὔ τᾶν ἕλοις ἥσσω   γε τῶν αἰσχρῶν ἐμέ.
   not, mark you would less (than), indeed shame, me
      you, find slave to dishonor

Η. ὁ γοῦν λόγος σοι πᾶς ὑπὲρ κείνης ὅδε.
   the at word, (to) you, every on that this
      least reason (of) you behalf of (girl)

Ι. καὶ σοῦ   γε κἀμοῦ, καὶ θεῶν τῶν νερτέρων.
   and (on behalf of) you indeed and me and the gods the infernal

CR. What! Is the city then to dictate how I must rule?

HAE. Don't you see you're talking like a child?

CR. Should I rule this land for others then and not for myself?

HAE. Yes, for it is no state if it belongs to a single person.

CR. Is not the state the ruler's possession?

HAE. You would make a good monarch of a desert.

CR. Obviously, he is in league with the woman.

HAE. If you are a woman. My whole concern is for you.

CR. You villain! to dispute your father's rights.

HAE. No, it's that I see you offending justice.

CR. Is it wrong for me to revere my kingly prerogatives?

HAE. You are not revering them when you trample on divine rights.

CR. You contemptuous woman's slave.

HAE. At least you will not find I'm a slave to dishonor.

CR. Your every word is for that girl.

HAE. Yes, and for you, for me, and for the gods below.

KP. ταύτην   ποτ'   οὐκ ἔσθ'   ὡς   ἔτι   ζῶσαν   γαμεῖς. 750
    her   ever, at   not it is   that still alive   you will
              any time   possible   marry

AI. ἣ   δ' οὖν   θανεῖται   καὶ θανοῦσ' ὀλεῖ   τινά.
    she well then she will die and dying   will destroy another

KP. ἦ κἀπαπειλῶν   ὧδ' ἐπεξέρχῃ   θρασύς;
    even threatening so do you proceed to the lengths,   rash(ly)
                         do you go to extremes

AI. τίς   δ'   ἔστ'   ἀπειλὴ   πρὸς   κενὰς γνώμας   λέγειν;
    what but is it   threat   against empty judgments to speak

KP. κλαίων   φρενώσεις,   ὧν   φρενῶν   αὐτὸς   κενός.
    weeping   you will   being of wisdom yourself   empty
    (i.e., at   make wise,
    your cost)   teach wisdom

AI. εἰ μὴ πατὴρ   ἦσθ',   εἶπον   ἄν σ' οὐκ εὖ   φρονεῖν. 755
    if not father you   I should   you not well,   to think
                   were   have said   rightly

KP. γυναικὸς   ὢν   δούλευμα,   μὴ   κώτιλλέ   με.
    of woman   being   chattel   do not tease, prattle, me
                                            wheedle, coax

AI. βούλῃ   λέγειν   τι   καὶ   λέγων   μηδὲν   κλύειν;
    do you   to say   something and   saying nothing   to hear
    wish   (in reply)

KP. ἄληθες;   ἀλλ' οὐ, τόνδ'   "Ολυμπον,   ἴσθ'   ὅτι,
    really?   but   not (by) this Olympus   know   that
    so?   (i.e., assuredly)

    χαίρων   ἐπὶ   ψόγοισι   δεννάσεις   ἐμέ.
    rejoicing   with   (continued)   you will revile me
    (with impunity)   censures

    ἄγετε τὸ   μῖσος,   ὡς   κατ'   ὄμματ'   αὐτίκα   760
    bring the hateful so   before (his very) immediately
    forth   thing   that   eyes

παρόντι   θνῄσκῃ   πλησία   τῷ   νυμφίῳ.
in the very presence   she may die   near   the   bridegroom

I. οὐ   δῆτ'   ἔμοιγε,   τοῦτο   μὴ   δόξῃς   ποτέ,
    not   indeed   (next to) <u>me</u>   this   do not   think   ever

οὔθ'   ἥδ'   ὀλεῖται   πλησία,   σύ   τ'   οὐδαμὰ
and not   she   will be destroyed,   near   you   and   never
                  will perish

τοὐμὸν   προσόψῃ   κρᾶτ'   ἐν   ὀφθαλμοῖς   ὁρῶν,
the my   you will see   head (i.e., me) with   eyes   seeing

ὡς   τοῖς   θέλουσι   τῶν   φίλων   μαίνῃ   συνών. 765
so   those consenting of the   friends you may   being
that   (i.e., your)   be mad   with

CR. You shall not ever marry her in this life.

HAE. She will die then and her death will destroy
another.

CR. How dare you threaten me?

HAE. What threat is it to contradict empty maxims?

CR. You will pay for teaching me wisdom, you empty fool.

HAE. If you were not my father, I would have said you
were the fool.

CR. Don't wheedle me, you woman's chattel.

HAE. You want to have your say but hear no reply?

CR. So? I swear you will not get away with these con-
tinuous insults. (To the guards) Bring out the hateful wretch
so that she may die next to her bridegroom, yes, before his
very eyes.

HAE. Not next to me--never think it--will she be
destroyed--and you will never lay eyes on me again. Go play
madman with such friends as will endure it.

THE ODE ON EROS: A TRANSLATION AND COMMENT

Strophe (781-90)

"O Eros unconquered in battle, Eros you who destroy men's
resources, Eros you who keep night watch on the soft cheek of
a maiden, you make your way over the deep sea and into wild
beasts' lairs. No immortal can escape you nor can ephemeral
man. And whoever possesses you is maddened."

Antistrophe (791-99)

"You lure even the just to injustice--to their own destruction. It is you too who have stirred up this strife among
kinsmen. The love glance that shines from the eyes of the fair
bride is victorious. That love is enthroned equally alongside
the great laws. For the unconquerable goddess Aphrodite
deceives her victims."

A recent critic argues that Creon's demand in the previous
episode that his servants "bring on the hated thing" (760)
results in Antigone's entrance onto stage on the heels of
Haemon's angry departure (766).[1] If so, she stands there as a
silent paradigm while the Chorus sings this short, suggestive
ode on the invincible power of Eros.[2]
The strophe of this ode, cast in hymnic form, sings common-
places about the militant love-god traditional in earlier lyric
poetry keeping "night watch on a young girl's soft cheek" and
maddening gods and men (783-90). The Chorus is, of course,
thinking of Haemon's great passion for Antigone, that invincible power which he suppressed until the end of the previous
scene when he threatened to die with her. These elders view
Eros through the lenses of the lyric poets: it is a bewitching,
undeniable spirit that no man or god can conquer.[3] The Chorus
lacks Sophocles' perception that the eros of Haemon for Antigone and the passions of Antigone are not enslaving but ennobling. The hymnic form suggests the new majesty with which

Sophocles is endowing the playful, dangerous god of earlier lyric poetry.

With the antistrophe, the Chorus takes us onto paths never before trodden by Hellenic lyricists. It portrays Eros as 1) a moral force, inciting kith against kin (794), 2) a power that sits enthroned as a peer alongside the "eternal laws" (797-98).[4] With the first insight (794), the Chorus is apparently reproaching the youthful Haemon for choosing his passion rather than his filial moral duty. Yet, the second insight (797) leads the audience to make a different application of the first. For by enthroning Eros alongside the "eternal laws" (797), the poet through his Chorus suggests that Eros is a moral force that both shares the rule with those unwritten laws of Antigone's defense (450-70) and gives that rule a proper balance.

This second insight of the poet, then, undercuts the Chorus's own belief that Eros lures "even the just to injustice" (791). The audience is thus invited to reflect on passion as another ennobling force alongside law. Neither eros nor law has driven either Haemon or Antigone to a morally false position; Haemon's eros, like Antigone's (see Guide, note on line 90), has not bewitched him into defending his guilty bride but into a willingness to share her innocent fate.

So the Chorus again inadvertently presents the poet's vision without understanding its application. It sings of love as a natural force and as a moral force, but it errs in believing the moral and natural aspects of love are mutually exclusive. Antigone's decision in the opening scenes to bury her brother flows from the moral power of eros; her words in the forthcoming lament bespeak her distress at the loss of the natural joys of eros. Similarly, Haemon has displayed the integrity of eros, the moral force, in his vain attempt to persuade his morally obtuse father. Finally, these two characters, ennobled by eros will find union only in the harbor of Hades (see 1284).

6

The Fourth and

Fifth Episodes

THE SETTING

The next selection, taken from Antigone's last speech (891-
928), comes from the concluding portion of the Fourth Episode.
There are two prior portions of the episode: Antigone's lament,
sung alternately with the Chorus (806-82), and Creon's brief
command that she be interred immediately (883-90). The theme
of desertion and isolation permeates her whole lament as she
concentrates now for the first time on the personal cost of her
act (813-70). Bereft of citizenship on earth and in the nether
world, isolated from family and friends, she pines mostly for
Haemon's love. She does not allow herself to mention him by
name, but her previously suppressed love now preoccupies her
lyrics (see the Introduction for her androgyny here). The
Chorus of elders now finally admits sympathy and questions the
morality of its own position (802-3). But it vacillates,
speaking alternately of her autonomy (821), her willfulness
(873-75), her rashness (853), and the reverence of her act
(872).

Creon's intervention (883-90) brings the lyrical lament to
an end and when Antigone speaks again (the passage below), it
is in spoken iambs, a mode more appropriate to analytic thinking than to emotional outbursts.

Critics have long questioned whether Sophocles wrote these
lines (at least 903-20). See the introduction to this passage
in the Guide for the various critical arguments and for my

reasons for retaining the passage as Sophoclean. Since, however, there is no compelling internal evidence, the student
must ultimately decide for himself whether the passage belongs
or not. However, given the manuscript tradition, the burden
of proof must be on those who would reject its authenticity.

ANTIGONE'S LAST SPEECH, 891-928

AN. ὦ   τύμβος,   ὦ   νυμφεῖον,   ὦ   κατασκαφῆς
O   tomb   O   bridal chamber   O   deeply dug, excavated

οἴκησις   αἰείφρουρος,   οἷ   πορεύομαι
house, dwelling ever-guarding (me) whither I go, am walking

πρὸς τοὺς   ἐμαυτῆς,   ὧν   ἀριθμὸν ἐν   νεκροῖς
to   those of me, myself   of whom number   among shades
            i.e., my own, my family

πλεῖστον   δέδεκται   Φερσέφασσ'   ὀλωλότων·
very great, most has received Persephone   of dead, perished

ὧν   λοισθία   'γὼ καὶ κάκιστα   δὴ   μακρῷ   895
of   left behind,   I   and the most   it would by far
whom last of all   miserable   seem

κάτειμι, πρίν μοι   μοῖραν   ἐξήκειν   βίου.
I go down before to me, alloted portion   to have ar-   of
              my   (of life)   rived, run out life

ἐλθοῦσα   μέντοι κάρτ'   ἐν   ἐλπίσιν τρέφω
going   yet   very much in,   hopes   I cherish,
                          among   nourish

φίλη μὲν ἥξειν   πατρί,   προσφιλὴς   δὲ   σοί,
dear   will come to (my) father dear, beloved and to you

μῆτερ, φίλη δὲ   σοί,   κασίγνητον   κάρα.
mother dear and to you brother   head, (i.e.,
                                        dear, very dear)

ἐπεὶ   θανόντας   αὐτόχειρ   ὑμᾶς   ἐγὼ   900
when   dead   working with   you   I
                  one's own hand

ἔλουσα   κἀκόσμησα   κἀπιτυμβίους
washed   and dressed, honored   and at your tombs

χοὰς	ἔδωκα·		νῦν	δέ,	Πολύνεικες,	τὸ	σὸν
libations	I offered (you)		now	and	Polynices	the	your

δέμας	περιστέλλουσα	τοιάδ᾽	ἄρνυμαι.
body	dress, wrap around, lay out	such	I receive, gain as a prize

καίτοι	σ᾽	ἐγὼ	'τίμησα	τοῖς	φρονοῦσιν	εὖ.
and yet	you	I	honored	those thinking		well, rightly (in the opinion of the wise)

οὐ	γάρ	ποτ᾽	οὔτ᾽	ἂν	εἰ	τέκνων	μήτηρ	ἔφυν	905
not	for	ever	neither		if	of children	mother	I had been	

οὔτ᾽	εἰ	πόσις	μοι	κατθανὼν	ἐτήκετο,
and not	if	husband	to me	having died, in death	lay mouldering, were wasting away

βίᾳ	πολιτῶν	τόνδ᾽	ἂν	ᾑρόμην	πόνον.
against the will of	the citizens	this		I should have undertaken	task

τίνος	νόμου	δὴ	ταῦτα	πρὸς	χάριν	λέγω;
what	principle, law	then, accordingly	these (things)	in compliance with, in deference to		do I say

AN. O tomb, O bridal chamber, O cavernous house that will
be my overseer forevermore. I journey now to meet my own,
since Persephone has received most of them among the ghosts of
the dead. To them I descend, the last remnant, most wretched
by far, to that realm before my portion of life has run out.
But as I go, I cherish the hope of being welcomed by you,
father, and by you, mother, and by you, dear brother. For when
you all lay dead, this hand of mine washed and dressed you and
offered libations at your graves. And now, Polynices, I
receive this reward for washing and dressing your body. And
yet, I was right in honoring you, as thoughtful men know. For
if I had lost sons, or if my husband lay wasting away in death,
I would never have undertaken this task against the city's
will. In accordance with what principle then, do I say this?

πόσις   μὲν   ἄν   μοι   κατθανόντος   ἄλλος   ἦν,
husband   to me   being dead   another   might be

καὶ   παῖς   ἀπ'   ἄλλου   φωτός,   εἰ   τοῦδ'   ἤμπλακον   910
and   child   from   another   man   if   this   I had lost

μητρὸς   δ'   ἐν   Ἅιδου   καὶ   πατρὸς   κεκευθότοιν
mother   but   in   Hades'   and   father   buried, being
                    (house)   concealed

οὐκ   ἔστ'   ἀδελφὸς   ὅστις   ἂν   βλάστοι   ποτέ.
not   is   brother   any who   could bud, bloom   ever

τοιῷδε   μέντοι   σ'   ἐκπροτιμήσασ'   ἐγὼ
by such   well   you   having selected   I
                        for special honor

νόμῳ,   Κρέοντι   ταῦτ'   ἔδοξ'   ἁμαρτάνειν
principle,   to Creon   (in) this   I seemed   to have acted
law   wrong, erred

καὶ   δεινὰ   τολμᾶν,   ὦ   κασίγνητον   κάρα.   915
and   terrible   to dare   O   brother   head,
      (things)   (i.e., dear)

καὶ   νῦν   ἄγει   με   διὰ   χερῶν   οὕτω   λαβὼν
and   now   he leads,   me   with   (violent)   thus   having
            drags   hands   seized

ἄλεκτρον,   ἀνυμέναιον,   οὔτε   του   γάμου
unwedded, without   without   neither   of any   marriage
bridal bed   bridal song

μέρος   λαχοῦσαν   οὔτε   παιδείου   τροφῆς,
portion   having obtained   nor   of children   rearing, nurture

ἀλλ'   ὧδ'   ἐρῆμος   πρὸς   φίλων   ἡ   δύσμορος
but   thus   deserted   by   dear (ones)   the   ill-fated

ζῶσ'	ἐς	θανόντων	ἔρχομαι	κατασκαφάς·	920
living	to	of the dead	I go	prisons, vaults, subterranean abodes	

ποίαν	παρεξελθοῦσα	δαιμόνων	δίκην;
what	having transgressed	of divine power, gods	law, justice

τί	χρή		με	τὴν	δύστηνον	ἐς	θεοὺς	ἔτι
why	is it necessary (i.e., of what use is it)		me	the	unhappy	to	gods	still

βλέπειν;	τίν'	αὐδᾶν	ξυμμάχων;	ἐπεί	γε δὴ
to look to, rely on	which (of the gods)	(can I) appeal to, invoke	as fighting along with, as allies	since	it would seem

τὴν	δυσσέβειαν	εὐσεβοῦσ'	ἐκτησάμην.
the	impiety, ungodliness	living reverently, by acting piously	I have got, gained, incurred

If my husband were dead there might be another, and another
child from another husband, if I had lost one. But now with
my father and mother both hidden in Hades, no brother could
ever blossom forth into life. Such is the principle, dear
brother, by which I have singled you out for special honor.
Yet Creon believes I have sinned in daring this terrible deed.
So now he has violently seized me and drags me off unwed,
without accompanying bridal song, without my share of marital
joy or motherhood. And so, it is my ill fate to descend to
the vaults of the dead while yet alive, utterly bereft of
those I love. What divine law have I transgressed? Why should
I continue to look to the gods in my desolation? Is there any
ally among the gods I could invoke, since by my piety I am
judged impious?

ἀλλ᾽   εἰ μὲν   οὖν   τάδ᾽   ἐστὶν   ἐν   θεοῖς   καλά, 925
but,   if   then   these,   is   in   gods   noble
well   this   (sight of)

παθόντες   ἂν ξυγγνοῖμεν   ἡμαρτηκότες·
(by) suffering,   I shall be   having missed the mark,
(in) suffering   conscious, come   sinned, gone amiss,
                           to know, confess   that I have sinned

εἰ   δ᾽   οἵδ᾽   ἁμαρτάνουσι,   μὴ   πλείω   κακὰ
if   but   these   go astray,   no   greater   evils
              (people)   are wrong

πάθοιεν   ἢ   καὶ   δρῶσιν   ἐκδίκως   ἐμέ.
may they suffer   than   also   they do lawlessly, unjustly   me

But if punishment has divine sanction, then through suffering,
I shall come to know my sin. But if it is they who are wrong,
may they suffer no greater evils than they lawlessly inflict
on me.

SUMMARY OF THE ACTION AND LYRICS
FROM ANTIGONE'S INTERNMENT TO THE EXODOS

The Ode on Mythological Prisoners (944-87). After the
guards remove Antigone, Creon hears the Chorus sing an ode
recalling three legendary figures who, like Antigone, endured
a rock-hewn prison. The Chorus dares not openly accuse the
powerful king, so it makes its judgment obliquely by alluding
to three famous mythological victims of cruelty, Danaë,
Lykurgos, and Kleopatra. The first and third are, like Antigone, innocent victims, but the one man, Lykurgos, is guilty
of true impiety. And since Lykurgos was a king, the spectators are invited to perceive an undeveloped similarity
between the legendary king and one standing before them.

The story of the third victim, Kleopatra, subtly suggests
both Antigone and Creon's wife, Eurydice, who will soon make
her brief appearance. Kleopatra's husband Phineus divorced
and imprisoned her so as to marry again. The Chorus sings of
the new wife's cruelty in blinding Kleopatra's two sons
(Eurydice will soon accuse Creon of destroying her two sons
Haemon and Megareus).

All are losers in this ode, the guilty Lykurgos and Phineus
and the innocent victims Danaë and Kleopatra. The dark, fore-
boding lyrics suggest the fates of Creon and Antigone, Haemon
and Eurydice. But the last phrase of the ode, "O child,"
shows that the Chorus's sympathy is now finally with the innocent youthful victims, Antigone and Haemon.

The Fifth Episode. In this episode (from which no bilingual
selection has been given), the incorruptible oracle of truth,
the aged Tiresias, gives the king his final chance. As Haemon
earlier brought word of the city's disapproval, Tiresias brings
word of divine disapproval. He tells of the rioting of the
augural birds, of multiple signs indicative of a godsent sick-
ness on the city resulting from Creon's inhumanity to his
nephew's corpse. But instead of following the seer's plea for
repentance, the king hears only Tiresias' mention of kerdos,
gain (1032), and launches in on another accusation of bribery,

this time of priestly bribery. At this, Tiresias and the
Chorus desert him. The seer's angry prophecy foretells the
king's doom and his son's death; he convicts Creon of two sins:
of consigning the living to the grave and of refusing burial to
the dead (1068 ff.). In his anger, the seer foretells political doom for Thebes: the cities whose sons share Polynices'
inhuman fate are about to seek vengeance on Creon's Thebes
(1077 ff.). Although the audience hardly notices this last
shaft from Tiresias' bow, Tiresias knows the tyrant well enough
to make it the climax of his argument. He then departs and
Creon makes an about-face unparalleled in any major Sophoclean character. In the manner and in words reminiscent of
Ismene in the Prologue, he acknowledges his impotence, asks
his subjects for guidance, and promises obedience (1099, cf.
67 and note on line 67 in the Guide).

As Creon departs, musing on "the established laws" (1113-
14), he has finally perceived the difference between true law,
nomos, and his own decree (cf. 481). He hurries off, then, to
execute his elders' counsel ("release the girl from her cell
and build a tomb for the outcast," 1100-1101). Creon, of
course, reverses the order, burying Polynices first and then
proceeding to the girl's tomb. The playwright gives no indi-
cation of the king's motivation. One is left to speculate as
to whether the reversal is due only to practical dramatic
needs, or whether Creon is still putting political expediency
above a person's welfare.

The Hymn to Dionysos (1115-54). The Chorus then sings a
joyous, confident hymn to Thebes' patron god, asking him to
heal the sick and to avert danger from the city. Although the
song celebrates Dionysos as the "god of many names" (i.e., the
bearer of life and of death, the donor of joy and of sorrow),
the ode accents the happy gifts. Paralleling the opening
parodos which also invoked Dionysos, there as lord of the dance
(153-54), this hymn with its lilting rhythms and joyful mood
heightens by contrast the spectators' sense of impending doom.

7

The Exodos

The Exodos or final movement of the play has two parts: the Messenger Scene, 1155-1256, and Creon's Lament, 1256-1353. In the first part, a messenger returning from Creon's side, gives a vivid account of the disasters he witnessed from within Antigone's stony prison. After some sermonizing on the caprices of fate, the messenger reports that Haemon is dead. Thereupon, Haemon's mother, Eurydice, suddenly makes her only appearance in the play and demands a full account of her son's death. Thus the story takes on an added pathos as the audience hears it from a mother's perspective. Creon's servants who had arrived at the cave before him, found Haemon wailing over the corpse of the girl who has hung herself. (The messenger never mentions "her" name--only a feminine adjective identifies the corpse as Antigone.) Then an anguished Creon rushed up to his son whose arms were around "her" waist. In response to a father's pleas, a bestial Haemon spat in his face and lunged at him--unsuccessfully--with his sword. Then, turning the blade upon himself, Haemon died embracing Antigone in pathetic consummation of the nuptial rites (1241). The messenger's woeful tidings now complete, the queen silently withdraws into the palace. Soon Creon and the audience are to hear of her suicide (1282-83).

Creon's final lament (1257-1353) records in Sophocles controlled manner Creon's bitter grief as he returns with his son's corpse and learns of his wife's accusatory suicide. The kommos is predominantly cast in the dochmiac meter, a meter reserved for moments of intense emotion.

The play ends with the choral "tag" (1347-53). While one should remember the obtuse character of the Chorus and thus avoid searching its final words for the play's "meaning", this tag does at least touch upon several of the key themes explored in the play. The final selection is the last seventy lines of the play.

CREON'S LAMENT, 1284-1353

ΚΡ. ἰώ,
    oh! alas!

ἰώ   δυσκάθαρτος   Ἅιδου   λιμήν,
alas! hard to purify,   of Hades, Death,   harbor, haven
       implacable, unexpiated nether world   of refuge

τί   μ'   ἄρα   τί   μ'   ὀλέκεις;   1285
why   me   then   why   me   do you ruin, destroy

ὦ   κακάγγελτά   μοι
O   tidings of dire woe   to me

προπέμψας   ἄχη,   τίνα   θροεῖς   λόγον;
escorting,   pains,   what   do you cry aloud,   message
bearer,   distress,   shriek forth
herald   sorrow

αἰαῖ,   ὀλωλότ'   ἄνδρ'   ἐπεξειργάσω.
alas! having perished, man   you have marched out against,
       come to an end   attacked, slain over again

τί   φής,   ὦ παῖ,   τίνα   λέγεις   μοι   νέον,
what do you say O slave   what   do you speak to me new, fresh

αἰαῖ   αἰαῖ,   1290
alas!   alas!

σφάγιον   ἐπ'   ὀλέθρῳ,
killing, slaying,   in addition to   destruction, ruin, death
violence

γυναικεῖον   ἀμφικεῖσθαι   μόρον;
woman's, wife's to lie about, over, be heaped on death, corpse

ΧΟ. ὁρᾶν   πάρεστιν·   οὐ   γὰρ   ἐν μυχοῖς   ἔτι.
    to see   it is at hand,   not   for   in inner chamber still
             evident   (i.e., within)

P. οἴμοι,
   woe to me! ah me!

κακὸν	τόδ᾽	ἄλλο	δεύτερον	βλέπω	τάλας.	1295
evil	this	other	second	I look at	wretched, foolish	

τίς	ἄρα, τίς	με	πότμος	ἔτι	περιμένει;
what	what	me	lot, destiny, evil destiny	yet	awaits

ἔχω	μὲν		ἐν	χείρεσσιν	ἀρτίως	τέκνον,
I have	on the one hand		in	(my) hands	just now	son

τάλας,	τὸν	δ᾽	ἔναντα	προσβλέπω	νεκρόν.
wretched	on the other hand	but	opposite	I see, look upon in addition	corpse

φεῦ	φεῦ	μᾶτερ	ἀθλία,		φεῦ	τέκνον. 1300
alas	alas	mother	subject to conflict, wretched		alas	son

(Creon speaking with a messenger who has just told him of
his wife's suicide within.)
    CR. Oh, inexorable harbor of Hades, why, oh why have you
destroyed me now? And you, herald of dire tidings, what is
your message of woe? Alas! You have slain me a second time!
Slave, what new horror do you announce? Alas! Is it death
upon death? A wife's cruel death too?
    CHO. It is here for you to see--it is no longer within.
(The corpse of Eurydice is wheeled out.)
    CR. Alas! I grieve to see this second, wretched evil.
What misfortune yet awaits me? Wretch that I am, I have just
now taken my son's body in my arms. Now I gaze upon this
second corpse. Oh, distressed mother! Oh, my son!

ΕΞΑΓΓΕΛΟΣ   MESSENGER

ἥ	δ'	ὀξύπληκτος		ἡμένη	δὲ	βωμία
she, this lady		struck by a sharp blow, goaded to despair		seated		at the altar, on the altar

λύει	κελαινὰ	βλέφαρα,	κωκύσασα		μὲν
relaxes, closes	black, dark, darkened	eyelids, eyes	having shrieked (over one's dead), having lamented		on the one hand

τοῦ	πρὶν	θανόντος	Μεγαρέως	κενὸν	λέχος,
the	before	having died	of Megareus	empty	bed

αὖθις	δὲ		τοῦδε,	λοίσθιον	δὲ	σοὶ	κακὰς
again, anew	on the other hand		of this one	lastly		you	bad, evil, base

πράξεις	ἐφυμνήσασα		τῷ	παιδοκτόνῳ.	1305
fortunes, exaction of vengeance	chanting repeatedly, imprecating, cursing		the	child-murderer, murderer of children	

ΚΡ. αἰαῖ   αἰαῖ

woe   woe

ἀνέπταν	φόβῳ.	τί	μ'	οὐκ	ἀνταίαν
I fly away, flutter, I am startled	with fear	why	me	not	full in front, opposite, hostile, fatal

ἔπαισέν	τις	ἀμφιθήκτῳ	ξίφει;
struck	someone	with double-edged	sword

δείλαιος		ἐγώ,	αἰαῖ,	1310
miserable, wretched		I	alas	

δειλαίᾳ	δὲ	συγκέκραμαι	δύᾳ.
wretched, sad		I am blended with, implicated in	misery, anguish, misfortune

Ξ. ὡς   αἰτίαν   γε   τῶνδε   κἀκείνων   ἔχων
   as   blame,   indeed   of this and of   bearing
          responsibility   that

   πρὸς   τῆς   θανούσης   τῆσδ'   ἐπεσκήπτου   μόρων.
   by   dead   this   you were denounced,   of the
                (woman)   accused   deaths

P. ποίῳ   δὲ   κἀπελύσατ'   ἐν   φοναῖς   τρόπῳ;
   in what   and did she   in, by bloodshed   manner
                 release herself   (i.e., bloody)

Ξ. παίσασ'   ὑφ'   ἧπαρ   αὐτόχειρ   αὐτήν,   ὅπως   1315
   striking   to,   liver (the own   herself when
              in the seat of the (violent)
              region of emotions) hand

   παιδὸς   τόδ'   ἤσθετ'   ὀξυκώκυτον   πάθος.
   of (her) this   she perceived, wailed with shrill   experience,
   son   heard   cries, lamented   misfortune

    ME. This distraught lady closed her dark eyes at the
altar. She wailed lamentation first over the empty bed of her
long dead Megareus and then over this son. Lastly, she called
down curses on you, the slayer of her sons.
    CR. Alas! I shudder with dread. Why has no one struck
me with a two-edged sword? A poor wretch, I am immersed in
wretched misfortune.
    ME. This dead woman cursed and blamed you for Haemon's
death and his brother's.
    CR. And how did she die?
    ME. With her own hand she struck her heart when she
heard the lament for Haemon's death.

KP. ὤμοι   μοι,   τάδ'   οὐκ ἐπ'   ἄλλον   βροτῶν
    alas   for me   these (things)   not to   another of mortals

    ἐμᾶς   ἁρμόσει   ποτ'   ἐξ   αἰτίας.
    my   will fit together,   ever   from   blame
             suit, adapt

    ἐγὼ   γάρ   σ'   ἐγὼ   'κανον,   ἰὼ   μέλεος,
    I   for   you   I   killed   oh   useless, unhappy

    ἐγώ,   φάμ'   ἔτυμον.   ἰὼ   πρόσπολοι,   1320
    I   I say   true, the truth   oh   servants, attendants

    ἀπάγετέ   μ'   ὅτι τάχος,   ἄγετέ   μ'   ἐκποδών,
    lead away   me   as quickly   lead   me   out of
                       as possible   the way

    τὸν   οὐκ ὄντα   μᾶλλον   ἢ   μηδένα.   1325
    the one   not being   more   than   (absolutely) nobody

XO. κέρδη   παραινεῖς,   εἴ τι   κέρδος ἐν κακοῖς·
    gains, profit you exhort, advise if any gain   in evils

    βράχιστα   γὰρ   κράτιστα   τἁν   ποσὶν   κακά.
    shortest   for   best   the before (our) feet   evils
                                    (i.e., demanding
                                    immediate attention)

KP. ἴτω   ἴτω,
    let it come   let it come

    φανήτω   μόρων   ὁ   κάλλιστ'   ἐμῶν
    let it   of fates,   the one   most happily   of my
    appear   of violent deaths

    ἐμοὶ   τερμίαν   ἄγων   ἁμέραν   1330
    to me   last   bringing   day

    ὕπατος·   ἴτω   ἴτω,
    highest, best,   let it come   let it come
    last, topmost

ὅπως   μηκέτ'   ἆμαρ   ἀλλ'   εἰσίδω.
so that   no longer   day   another   I may see

O. μέλλοντα   ταῦτα.   τῶν   προκειμένων τι   χρὴ
are in the   these   of the   lying   something it is
future   (things)   (matters) before (us)   necessary

πράσσειν. μέλει γὰρ τῶνδ' ὅτοισι   χρὴ   μέλειν. 1335
to do   it is for of   to (those) it is   to be
          concern   these whom   necessary   concerned

P. ἀλλ'   ὧν   ἐρῶμεν   ταῦτα   συγκατηυξάμην.
at least,   which   we (I) desire these   I have summed up
still   passionately   (things)   in my prayer

O. μή   νυν   προσεύχου   μηδέν·   ὡς   πεπρωμένης
no   pray, make prayer   nothing   fated, destined

οὐκ   ἔστι   θνητοῖς   συμφορᾶς   ἀπαλλαγή.
not   is   for mortals   fortune,   deliverance,
                             misfortune   means of escape

CR. Woe! The guilt falls on me--on no one else. Unhap-
pily, it is I, I who killed you. I speak the truth. Servants,
take me away, take me out of sight quickly. I am worth nothing
at all.

CHO. You advise profitably, if there can be profit in
such adversity. Brevity is best amid sorrows.

CR. Let it come! Let it come! Let my last day bring
the most fortunate violence of death. Let it come! Let it
come! May I never see another day.

CHO. That is in the future. The present must be our
concern. Others must decide what is to come.

CR. That prayer of mine contains all my wishes.

CHO. Pray no more now. For mortals have no escape from
their destinies.

KP. ἄγοιτ᾽ ἂν   μάταιον   ἄνδρ᾽ ἐκποδών,

    lead, conduct   empty, rash,   man   out of the
    if you please   foolish   way

ὃς, ὦ παῖ, σέ τ᾽ οὐχ ἑκὼν   κατέκανον 1340

who O son   you both not willingly, purposely,   I killed
                               wittingly

σέ   τ᾽ αὖ τάνδ᾽,   ὤμοι μέλεος,   οὐδ᾽ ἔχω

you and too this one alas wretched not I possess mentally,
                                             understand, know

πρὸς   πότερον   ἴδω,   πᾷ   κλιθῶ·   πάντα   γὰρ

toward   which of   I should in which I should   all   for
         the two   look   way   lean, rely (things)

λέχρια   τάν   χεροῖν, τὰ   δ᾽   ἐπὶ κρατί μοι 1345

aslant,   these (my)   those   but upon head   me
awry, prone in,   hands   (things)
(of corpse) these things
             in my hands

πότμος   δυσκόμιστος   εἰσήλατο.

lot,   unbearable   has sprung into,
destiny   has leaped down

XO. πολλῷ   τὸ   φρονεῖν   εὐδαιμονίας

    by far   to have understanding   of prosperity, good
               (i.e., discretion, wisdom)   fortune, happiness

πρῶτον   ὑπάρχει· χρὴ   δὲ τά   γ᾽   ἐς θεοὺς

the very first, is   it is   and the   indeed to gods
primal,   necessary (things)
principal   (what concerns the gods)

μηδὲν   ἀσεπτεῖν·   μεγάλοι δὲ λόγοι   1350

not at all,   to be impious, great,   and words,
not by any means   to slight   haughty   language

μεγάλας   πληγὰς   τῶν   ὑπεραύχων

great, large   blows   overboastful, overproud

ἀποτείσαντες
(by) repaying, paying the debt, atoning for

γήρᾳ   τὸ   φρονεῖν   ἐδίδαξαν.
in old age,   to understand   teach
lately, finally   (i.e., wisdom)

CR. Lead me out of sight, a poor empty fool. Unwittingly, I killed you, my son, and you, my wife. Wretch that
I am, I know not where to look or where to lean for support.
Everything I have touched, both here and there, is awry. An
unbearable fate has crashed down upon me. (He is taken
within.)

CHO. Wisdom is the very core of happiness. One may
never slight the gods. Haughty words inflict heavy blows upon
the proud. And these teach wisdom at long last.

GRAMMATICAL APPENDIX

NOTES

GRAMMATICAL APPENDIX

As the Preface noted, this Appendix is modest in scope and purpose. It is not an introduction to Greek grammar or to Sophoclean style. Instead, it presumes some linguistic sophistication and attempts to discuss some of the ways the Greek verb differs from its English counterpart and some of the differences in usage of the Greek article and adjective. It also gives the personal endings of the most commonly used verbs and describes a few unfamiliar grammatical terms. These rudimentary aids should help the student grapple with the bilingual text and should prepare him for the more technical Grammatical Notes and Vocabulary of the Guide. This Appendix, however, will have really served its purpose when the student realizes its limitations and turns to a standard grammar or enrolls in a course in elementary Greek.

THE VERB

Moods: The Subjunctive and Optative

In addition to the indicative mood (most commonly used in simple absolute statements and questions) and the imperative mood (used in commands and prohibitions), Greek has the subjunctive and optative moods. The subjunctive is used independently in exhortations (1332) and in some prohibitions (649); the optative is used independently in wishes (928) and in sentences expressing a future possibility--such sentences also

include the particle an (680, 731); line 686 exhibits both of
these independent usages of the optative: "I would not be able
to say--may I not learn how to."

In certain dependent clauses (e.g., expressing purpose, con-
dition etc.), these two moods are also used. In such sentences, the subjunctive is normally employed when the main verb
is in the present or future tense; and the optative is substi-
tuted after main verbs in the past tenses. In purpose clauses,
for instance, the subjunctive is normally found where English
has "may," and the optative where English has "might." The
underlined verb in the following sentence is in the subjunctive
mood: "Men pray for worthy children...so that they may honor
their father's friends" (641-44).

Voices: The Middle Voice

In addition to the usual active and passive voices, Greek
uses the middle voice when the subject acts upon itself, or
acts in a way that concerns its own advantage or disadvantage,
e.g., edidaxato, "he taught himself" (354), and pepausomai,
"I shall stop (myself)" (91). Since the passive voice borrows
the forms of the middle voice in all tenses except the future
and aorist, context and the Grammatical Notes of the Guide will
help the reader distinguish one from the other. Not all verbs
have all voices. In fact, some verbs are "deponent," i.e.,
they are middle or passive in some or all forms but active in
meaning (e.g., erchomai, "I come," and keimai, "I lie").

Tenses: The Aorist

The aorist tense indicates instantaneous action in past time
and is often described as "the snapshot tense" in contrast to
"the motion picture tenses," i.e., the present and imperfect.
The latter tenses express continued or habitual action in present and past times respectively, but the aorist is the tense
for simple action in past time (e.g., "I did it," "he
announced"). The perfect tense is distinct from the aorist in
that it denotes the permanent result of a past action in the

present (e.g., "she is dead").

The distinction between the so-called first and second aorist is generally restricted to formation and thus does not normally affect the meaning.

The Infinitive

As in English, the infinitive is commonly used to complete a verb (e.g., "Do you intend to bury him?"). Two other common uses of the Greek infinitive are:

a) In an infinitive phrase used as the object of a verb of mental action--e.g., "I think him to be wise," i.e., "I think that he is wise." This use is called indirect discourse. See e.g., 31-36, 452-53, 460, 775. In the example at 31-36, four infinitives depend on the one verb of mental action, phasi, "they say."

b) With a neuter article, used like any neuter noun--i.e., as subject or object of a verb, as object of a preposition: e.g., "wisdom is the foundation of happiness" (1348); "wisdom" here is to phronein, lit., "the to be wise"; similarly to... perissa prassein (67-68); in both cases the infinitive phrase is subject of the verb, and the neuter nominative article, to, is the clue to the case of the infinitive. Such infinitives are most often in the nominative case, but at 1353 to phronein is the direct object of the verb.

The Participle

The participle has two principal uses:

a) Attributive--i.e., modifying a noun or pronoun like any adjective (e.g., see 22, 26, 30, 46, 65, 72); when used with an article, such a participle is equivalent to a noun, e.g., tois phronousin eu (904), lit., "to the thinking well (ones)," i.e., "to the wise"; cf. also 94.

b) Circumstantial--i.e., defining the circumstances under which an action occurs. This second use is very common in all Greek authors; where English idiom uses a relative or adverbial clause (when, since, although, etc.) or even a correlative clause, Greek commonly uses a circumstantial participle, e.g., _pathontes_ (926), lit., "suffering," i.e., "when we have suffered"; _elthousa...trephō_, lit., "going...I nourish," i.e., "as I go," or "when I go, I nourish" (897).

FORM OF THE VERB

Elements: Root, Infix, Ending, and Augment

Every verb-form has at least two elements, a root and an ending--e.g., _leg-ō_, "I say," _leg-ei_, "he," "she," or "it says"; most have three or more elements--e.g., _leg-o-men_, "we say," _leg-e-te_, "you say," the infix o/e serving both to indicate tense and mood and as a connector between the root of the word and the ending; _e-leg-on_, "I was saying," or "they were saying"; the augment--i.e., the letter, _epsilon_, prefixed to the word, serves as a signal for a past tense. The letter _epsilon_ is the usual augment; however, for words beginning with vowels, the augment normally consists of a lengthening of the initial vowel, e.g., _omicron_, a short _o_, becomes _ōmega_, a long _ō_ in the imperfect or aorist, e.g., _ōrthou_ (167) and _ōrthosan_ (163) are imperfect and aorist forms respectively of _orthoō_; the augment is added to the root of the verb, not to prepositional prefixes, e.g., _eis-e-ballon_, _hyp-e-graphon_. Contraction sometimes hides augment: e.g., _proupempon_ is the contracted form of _pro-e-pempon_. Since the augment is a time-indicator, it is found regularly only in the indicative mood.

Principal Parts

The principal parts of a verb are the first person singular indicative forms of the various tense-systems. A regular verb has six principal parts, i.e., the first person singular indicative of the following: present, future, aorist active, perfect active, perfect middle, and aorist passive.

Personal Endings of O-Verbs

Verb tenses are classified as primary (present, future, and perfect) and secondary or historical (imperfect, aorist, and pluperfect).

a) Primary personal endings are used in the primary tenses and, in a lengthened form, in the subjunctive. The infixes, plus primary endings, in their most common form are:

Active Voice		Middle and Passive	
Sing.	Pl.	Sing.	Pl.
1. -ω	-ομεν	-ομαι	-όμεϑα
2. -εις	-ετε	-ει	-εσϑε
3. -ει	-ουσι(ν)	-εται	-ονται

b) The infixes plus the secondary endings are used in the secondary or past tenses of the indicative and, with some variations, in the optative:

Active Voice		Middle and Passive Voice	
Sing.	Pl.	Sing.	Pl.
1. -ον	-ομεν	-όμην	-όμεϑα (όμεσϑα)
2. -ες	-ετε	-ου	-εσϑε
3. -ε(ν)	-ον	-ετο	-οντο

The so-called first or weak aorist is recognizable by its tense sign, the letter alpha which combines with the secondary endings as follows:

Active Voice		Middle Voice	
Sing.	Pl.	Sing.	Pl.
1. -α	-αμεν	-άμην	-άμεϑα
2. -ας	-ατε	-ω	-ασϑε
3. -ε(ν)	-αν	-ατο	-αντο

The most common aorist passive stem is recognizable by the
addition of a thēta. Perfect tenses are usually recognizable
by the presence of a reduplicated stem. The most common form
of reduplication is a doubling of the initial consonant of the
root and a joining of that letter to the root with an epsilon,
e.g., pepauka, leluka from pauō and luō respectively. All
aorist passives and perfect tenses are identified in the
Grammatical Notes of the Guide.

The endings given above belong only to the most common,
regular O verbs. Another class of verbs, few in number but in
common usage, end in -mi in the first person singular. The
forms of these verbs are all identified in the Grammatical
Notes.

USES AND POSITIONS OF ARTICLES, ADJECTIVES, AND ADVERBS

The definite article serves approximately the same role in
Greek as in English. One particular use, however, is far more
common in Greek. Articles with adjectives or participles give
the latter a substantive force--e.g., tous kakous, "the evil
(ones)," "the wicked"; pros tous emautou, lit., "to those of
me," i.e., "to my family"; tōn olōlotōn, "of the dead" (174);
this substantival use of adjectives is particularly common with
the neuter adjective or participle to express general abstract
notions that the mind was forming--e.g., to deinon, "the dreadful thing," to mēchanoen technās, "the inventiveness of art"
(365).

Adverbs placed between articles and their nouns have the
force of attributive adjectives, e.g., tōn katō theōn, lit.,
"of the below gods," i.e., "the infernal gods" or "the gods who
dwell below."

SOME UNFAMILIAR GRAMMATICAL TERMS

Augment: See Form of the Verb above.

Crasis and Elision: When a word that ends with a vowel pre-
cedes a word that begins with a vowel, one of two processes may
occur:

1) The final short vowel of the first word may fall away
(elision) and an apostrophe marks the omission--e.g., in lines
2 and 4; the presence of an initial aspirate (rough breathing)
is indicated by substituting the aspirated form of a final pi,
tau, or kappa--e.g., kata hēmerān--is written kath' hēmerān
(171); malista hadein is malisth' hadein (89);

2) The two vowels may combine (a process called "crasis,"
lit., a "mixing") and the two words are written as one--e.g.,
kautōi for kai autōi; see also 1345; the word, kai commonly
undergoes crasis.

In the transliterations of this text and in the Grammatical
Notes and Commentary of the Guide, the full form of such words
and phrases is given by adding the omitted vowel(s) in paren-
theses--e.g., kat(a) or ta (e)n cheroin.

Deponent Verbs: See Middle Voice above.

Dual Number: In addition to the usual singular and plural,
early Greek had a dual number, used when reference was being
made to two persons or things which by nature or association
formed a pair. Although the dual was rare in Sophocles' time,
he employed it with peculiar effectiveness in the Prologue
(e.g., 3, 13, 21 etc.; see Guide, note on lines 2-3).

Particles: Broadly considered, particles include all words
in the Greek sentence that are not nouns, adjectives, pronouns,
or verbs; i.e., adverbs, prepositions, conjunctions, and inter-
jections. In a more narrow sense, however, the term "particle," is used to identify that large number of "sentence adverbs" that is peculiarly Greek. J. O. Denniston defines a
particle in this more narrow sense as "a word expressing a mode
of thought, considered either in isolation or in relation to
another thought, or a mood of emotion" (The Greek Particles
[Oxford: Clarendon, 1954], p.xxxviii). Sentences, clauses,
phrases, and single words are usually linked by a connecting
particle to the preceding unit. These often untranslatable
little words subtly show the relation between ideas. Especially at the beginning of a new thought and at moments of ex-
citement and emotional tension, these words abound. Denniston
(p.lxxiii) suggests that women were particularly addicted to
their use "just as women today are fond of underlining words in

their letters." To be more precise, perhaps one should say
that the frequency of such words in women's speeches indicates
that the dramatists thought women were so addicted.

Particles are often important in establishing the tone or
emphasis in a sentence. Some turn statements into questions,
some throw emphasis onto the preceding word (e.g., ge, 214),
some are strongly adversative (e.g., alla, "but"), some are
weakly adversative and often better left untranslated (e.g.,
de). Sophocles, with his highly antithetical style, achieves
subtle effects with the common particles, men...de, the pair
of particles that places two words, phrases, clauses, or sentences in antithetical balance. See e.g., 22, 165 ff., 194
ff., 1298-99, and the introduction to the "Prologue", chap. 1,
in the Guide. The interlinear English often renders men, "on
the one hand," and de, "on the other hand," but this over-
translates the unobtrusive particles. Like most particles
(e.g., toi, ara, ge), men and de are light delicate words whose
force is often best rendered by a tonal inflection, a pause or
a stress rather than a word. Thus, in the translation, italics
are sometimes used to convey the force of a particle.

NOTES

PREFACE

1.   Joan V. O'Brien, Guide to Sophocles' "Antigone": A
Student Edition with Commentary, Grammatical Notes, and
Vocabulary (Carbondale and Edwardsville: Southern Illinois
University Press, 1977). Hereafter cited as Guide. See C. J.
Herington's "Classical Commentaries for Our Time: A Proposal,"
Arion 7 (1968): 558-68. Herington proposed a text in which a
Greek prose paraphrase would appear side by side with the
classical Greek text. In this bilingual text and in the
Guide, I have changed Herington's original proposal beyond
recognition, but I am grateful to him for helpful suggestions
and encouragement.
2.   I have, with few exceptions, used the text of the play
as edited by A. C. Pearson (Sophoclis Fabulae [1924; reprint
ed., Oxford: Clarendon, 1955]). Although I have not concen-
trated on textual problems, I have noted in the Commentary of
the Guide where and why I adopt different readings from those
of Pearson for these selections (e.g., at 213, 368-69, 663-67,
718, 1314). For a text with English translation and notes,
see Sir Richard Jebb, ed., Sophocles: The Plays and Fragments,
pt.3, The Antigone, 2d ed. (1891; reprint ed., Cambridge:
University Press, 1928); Jebb's text is also available in
E. S. Shuckburgh's abridged version The Antigone of Sophocles
11th ed. (New York: Cambridge University Press, 1971). For
other editions and for other general bibliography, see the
Guide. Since the bibliography there is extensive, this text
includes no general bibliography.
3.   For a comprehensive grammar, see H. W. Smyth, Greek
Grammar, rev. G. M. Messing (1956; reprint ed., Cambridge,
Mass.: Harvard University Press, 1974).
4.   The Guide is built around the same seven passages as
this text is. The Guide, however, does not provide the actual
passage but gives a line-by-line commentary on the relevant
literary, philosophical, and cultural background; there are
also grammatical aids for each passage. There are other aids
in the Guide that the ambitious Greekless reader can consult:
introductions to Sophocles' diction and thought, a Vocabulary

(more elaborate than usual for the sake of the novice), a
Selected Bibliography, two appendixes (one on the chronology
of the poet's life, the other on his relation to the Theban
myths).

INTRODUCTION: ANDROGYNY IN THE ANTIGONE

1. Although I had reached my own conclusions about Antigone's "masculine" and "feminine" wholeness before reading
Carolyn Heilbrun's fascinating study, Toward a Recognition of
Androgyny (New York: Knopf, 1973), I borrowed the term, androgyny, from her. Heilbrun finds three androgynous elements in
Antigone: the inversion of traditional roles in Antigone and
Haemon, the contrast between Antigone and Ismene, and the
androgynous Tiresias. I discount the last element since Sophocles makes nothing of the androgynous element in the Tiresias
myth, and I try to show that the other androgynous elements
are more complex and profound than Heilbrun perceives. Also,
she errs, I believe, in assuming that androgyny in Greece was
connected with the fact that early Greeks were not yet wholly
cut off from their matriarchal origins. First of all, Sophocles, writing in fifth-century Athens, was a long remove from
any matriarchal past. But more important, the male triumph
over matriarchy (mythically represented by the Olympian revo-
lution over the earlier "chthonic" female gods) did not
bequeath androgyny to Greece but a strong male fear and preju-
dice against female power. See E. A. S. Butterworth, Some
Traces of the Pre-Olympian World in Greek Literature and Myth
(Berlin: DeGruyter and Co., 1966), chap.1, "The Matrilineal
World."
2. Critics have always pondered the paradoxical fact that
male-dominated Athens produced some of drama's strongest
heroines. (See Guide, note on lines 678-80).
All three tragedians created great women. Why Sophocles
should have been the one to achieve androgynous wholeness in
Antigone is hard to say, although certain historical conditions
helped. On the one hand, the years in which he wrote the Ajax
and the Antigone coincide with the passionate concern about
man, "the measure of all things." The Sophist Protagoras, to
whom this saying is attributed, came to Athens a year or two
before the production of the Antigone. While Aeschylus, Sophocles' older contemporary, felt the impulse of the anthropocen-
trism, the emphasis in the early stages of this movement was on
seeing man's relation to divinity and, in the plastic arts at
least, on discovering the male of the species. On the other
hand, although Euripides is Sophocles' younger contemporary, in
spirit the two men belong to different ages. Sophocles imbibed
the confidence of the years of Athenian ascendancy after the
Greeks had turned back the tyrant, Persia. His characters,
then, possess a wholeness generally missing in Euripidean
antagonists. The younger playwright felt the decay and cyni-
cism of the coming age with prophetic insight. So, despite
Euripides' empathy for women, his characters, whether male or
female, are usually too fragmented to be androgynous by my
definition.

Thus, it seems to me (and I emphasize the subjective nature of this judgment), neither Aeschylus' Clytemnestra with her "heart of manly purpose" (Aeschylus Agamemnon 11) nor Euripides' magnificent Medea exhibits a human wholeness basic to my definition of androgyny. Both are magnificent creations and it is doubtful that all literature has produced more dominant women. However, Aeschylus portrays Clytemnestra as a perversion of her sex; and Medea's passion finally destroys her humanity. Phaedra in the Hippolytos is often called the most "whole" of Euripides' heroines but her strength lies in the "feminine" sphere. The Oceanids in Prometheus Bound anticipate Antigone's noble rebellion from the status quo, but they rebel in following Prometheus rather than as initiating heroines.

The best source for androgynous women in the pre-Greek ancient world is the Hebrew Bible. A biblical character that offers some interesting parallels to Antigone is the widow Tamar in Genesis 38. When denied her legal right of offspring, Tamar takes the law into her own hands, disguises as a temple prostitute, and tricks her unsuspecting father-in-law into fathering her twins. Temple prostitution was a heinous crime in her society; yet the narrator allows the story to show his admiration for her courageous initiative and her moral superiority to her father-in-law. Although the context and purpose of the story is far removed from the context and purpose of Sophocles' drama, Antigone and Tamar both show courage in using unorthodox and hazardous means of carrying out the "spirit" of the law. Like Antigone, Tamar dared to commit a "criminal" act that might result in her death; and she reveals her moral superiority to her male adversary who is both the legal authority and a relative.

3. This is my judgment, not Heilbrun's. In makeup these two young girls are miles apart. Shaw's Joan is more overtly political, is antifeminine and militant ("I am a soldier: I do not want to be thought of as a woman. I will not dress as a woman"); and her rebellion is more sweeping (the chaplain exaggerates but accurately represents the public's view when he says she rebels against the church, against God, and against England). However, in her deep conviction that she is right and in her willingness to die for that conviction ("I shall dare, dare and dare again in God's name"), Joan exhibits an androgynous strength quite reminiscent of Antigone. Interestingly, too, Joan's conviction, like Antigone's survives and is strengthened by a momentary loss of perspective (in Joan's case, it involves an actual recantation). Shaw's words about his heroine could be applied with some reservation to Antigone: "But marriage...pursuit and capture of a husband was not her business: she had something else to do. [In Antigone's case, however, she did not want to reject marriage.] Byron's formula, 'Man's love is of man's life a thing apart: 'tis woman's whole existence' did not apply to her any more than to George Washington or any other masculine worker on the heroic scale" (G. B. Shaw, Saint Joan [Leipzig: Bernhard Tauchnitz, 1924], Preface, p. 16). Similarly, Heilbrun's conclusion (p. 111) about Joan holds true for Antigone; i.e., that Joan is an "entirely androgynous figure" because Shaw was able "to portray in one person a female being with masculine aptitudes, who...

reminded humanity of the need for feminine impulses in the
world." Perhaps a full-scale comparison of these two androgynous figures would reveal that Antigone's character reveals
a "balanced poise" between "feminine" and "masculine" traits
missing in Joan, but it would not dispute the androgyny of
either character.

4. See Carl G. Jung et al, Man and His Symbols (New York:
Doubleday, 1964), especially M. L. von Franz, "The Process of
Individuation," pp. 118-229, for a description of the anima
(personification of "all feminine psychological tendencies,
such as vague feelings and moods, prophetic hunches, recep-
tiveness to the irrational, capacity for personal love, feeling
for nature and...relation to the unconscious") and the animus
(personification of "an enterprising spirit, courage, truthful-
ness and, in the highest form, spiritual profundity"). In a
telephone conversation, Daniel Levinson, social psychologist
at Yale, said these traditional "masculine" and "feminine"
categories seem to be fairly accurate descriptions of young
males and females, that young adults normally split off the
qualities associated with the other sex until they become
secure in their own sexual identity: therefore he believes
androgyny is not normally possible before middle life.

5. Ajax's monologue (Ajax 646-92) in which he seems to submit has been variously interpreted. See Appendix D in W. B.
Stanford, ed., Sophocles' Ajax (New York: St. Martin's Press,
1963) for different interpretations.

6. In the introduction to the "Prologue" in the Guide
(chap. 1) I note how Sophocles uses a verbal coincidence to
dramatize Antigone's rejection of Ismene's obedience. Two
very different words just happen to have the same form,
peisomai, in the future tense. Ismene's peisomai, "I shall
obey," is followed by Antigone's peisomai, "I shall not suffer
anything so terrible as an ignoble death."

7. B. M. W. Knox, The Heroic Temper: Studies in Sophoclean
Tragedy, Sather Series 35 (Berkeley: University of California
1964), p. 52.

8. Thomas Henn, Harvest of Tragedy (New York: Barnes and
Noble, 1966), p. 122. Henn adds: "But the true woman's part,
in high tragedy, is beyond all doubt to mirror the perfection
of selfless love." And again, "She [Cordelia in King Lear] is
the pattern of the love that delivers from evil; she alone has
the power to suffer all extremity without yielding to pain."
She manifests "the multiple emotions of joy, tenderness, the
largesse of the spirit, the essential gentleness."

9. See Guide, note on line 91, on the effect of this rare
verb form: a future perfect, in the middle voice. See the
Grammatical Appendix for the force of the middle voice.

10. See Guide, chap. 6, introduction to "Antigone's Last
Speech," for differing critical views on this; I also note
there that Antigone in this passage combines emotional "feminine" logic with the cool "masculine" devices of rationalism,
and the "masculine" iambic meter appropriate for discursive
analysis.

11. Antigone's unwritten laws play a far less prominent role
in her motivation than Joan's "voices" do. This is entirely
in keeping with Sophocles' usual ambiguity and understatement
in reference to divinity. See the Ode on Atē, chap. 4, and

the comment there.

12. My translation of the second half of line 939 may involve an overtranslation. It may simply mean: "I no longer delay." But even so, my interpretation of the line is still possible, although it differs from that of other commentators. Jebb takes the phrase as a statement of the obvious: "I am no longer (merely) about to be led away." Seyffert, an older commentator, takes it as a firm, proud statement of the fact that she will not bring punishment on her guards by delaying them longer. Jebb objects to Seyffert's translation as inappropriate for agomai dē. But if agomai dē refers to the ancestral gods as I suggest, the line is firm and proud, as Seyffert suggested, but for a different reason.

13. Limitations of space prevent me from discussing the quite different but equally strong pity and horror Ajax elicits. For a short but fine analysis of this, see David Grene's "Ajax," pp. 118-36, in his Reality and the Heroic Pattern (Chicago: University of Chicago Press, 1967).

14. James Joyce, A Portrait of the Artist as a Young Man (New York: B. W. Huebsch, 1916), p. 239.

15. See Guide, note on line 74, for the pejorative ring usually evident in the uses of panourgein.

16. Simone de Beauvoir, The Second Sex, trans. H. M. Parshley (New York: Modern Library, 1968), p. 661. Beauvoir also adds: "to forget oneself it is first of all necessary to be firmly assured that now and for the future one has found herself." See also Heilbrun (p. 99) where she cites Adele Quested in E. M. Forster's A Passage to India for performing "the one act most difficult for us all: she makes a fool of herself in the cause of justice. She does this, moreover, in a public act."

17. On the limits of that altruism and on the distinction between Antigone's altruism, philia, and the Judaeo-Christian use of agapē, see J. O'Brien, "Sophocles' Ode on Man and Paul's Hymn on Love: A Comparative Study," Classical Journal 71 (1975-76): 138-51.

18. See Guide, chap. 1, introduction to the "Prologue," and note on lines 88-93.

19. See the introduction to the "Ode on Man" in the Guide (chap. 3) for Sophocles' use of the Chorus with its limited perspective as an ironic persona for his own deeper insights. See also the bibliography there for other treatments of this many faceted ode.

20. See Guide, note on lines 337-38, for another feminine image in the first strophe, that of Mother Earth.

21. Marc Fasteau, The Male Machine (New York: McGraw-Hill, 1974), p. 197.

22. See n. 4 above.

23. See Creon's speech, 639-80, for an oligarchic and tyrannical view of law and Haemon's reply, 683-723, as an argument for democratic participation and development of a consensus.

24. E.g., Haemon uses images of light for Antigone and of darkness for Creon (690-704), but his diplomatic handling of the "darkening rumor" shows his sincere desire to remove the gloomy implications from his father.

25. See Guide, note on line 718, where I explain why I do not follow Pearson's reading on this line.

26. Although this omission is much lamented by Victorian scholars and even some recent critics, there is no reason to search for abstruse reasons as the French critic Méautis does when he suggests that the omission is due to a sense of shame which prevented Greek women from avowals of love. Clearly, the dramatic need to isolate Antigone from any human support made any such encounter unthinkable. Euripides, however, wrote an Antigone (it has not survived) in which her love for Haemon was evidently dramatized.

27. See William M. Calder III, "Sophocles' Political tragedy, Antigone," Greek Roman and Byzantine Studies 9 (1968): 399, for a very different reading of the relationship (and of the play). He contrasts Haemon's friendly but reasoned dissent with "the hysteria of Antigone."

28. Haemon's very name (haima, "blood") suggests the primacy of blood relationships over the rights of the polis. See note on line 659 in the Guide.

29. Both Jebb and Pearson give the line to Antigone against the manuscript tradition. See H. D. F. Kitto's discussion of the question and his reason for siding with Jebb and Pearson in Form and Meaning in Drama (London: Methuen, 1959), pp. 162-63. I reject the tampering with the text because such a fragmentary expression of Antigone's love would be a dubious gain, because stichomythia (dialogue in which single lines are spoken by alternate speakers) is not usually interrupted by a third party, but also because the separate characterization of the two lovers is much more suggestive of what might have been than any interjection of "dearest" on Antigone's part.

30. The word harmozdein was used musically to express a spiritually or aesthetically pleasing harmony of diverse elements. It may be significant that the only other use of the word in the play occurs when Creon finally sees that the only thing that can be "joined" or "adapted" to him is guilt (1318).

31. See the Oedipus at Kolonos where the aged Sophocles develops the loving side of Antigone's nature. Obviously, that play with its scenes between Oedipus and Antigone allowed more scope for her affection to display itself. Also she finally promises in that play to yield (Oedipus at Kolonos 1769). It may be that the poet felt the need to show his heroine in a less harsh light than the nature of the Antigone allowed. Like Haemon in this play, the Antigone of Oedipus at Kolonos seems "gynecandrous."

4 THE SECOND EPISODE AND THE ODE ON ATĒ

1. The problem of the double burial has confounded critics. Why, in addition to the obvious dramatic gain, did the playwright construct his plot around two burials? A recent commentator, Marsh McCall, "Divine and Human Action in Sophocles," Yale Classical Studies 22 (1972): 105-12, summarizes the various critical judgments; among the most convincing are 1) it is simply the response of her love that makes her return to her brother's body when she learned it was uncovered; 2) the two burials allow the audience to see her triumph before her defeat; 3) the first burial was as the Chorus suggested: a

divine burial; Zeus protected Polynices as he had Sarpedon in the Iliad. This last argument is McCall's own position, for which he argues with much cogency, especially on the grounds that the same word, theēlaton, "god-driven," is used in the Iliad (16. 667) of Zeus' burial of Sarpedon. Most critics would not go that far, but they do agree that there is in the burial and in the play an intermingling of divine and human motivation and action.

2. See E. R. Dodds, The Greeks and the Irrational (pp. 37 ff.) for the history of atē and interpretations of it. In Homer, atē is a cloud of confusion, delusion, or infatuation temporarily destroying a person's judgment. At Iliad 19. 91 ff., atē is personified as the elder daughter of Zeus who blinds (aātai) man and leads him astray.

3. Richard Emil Braun, Sophocles' Antigone (New York: Oxford University Press, 1973), p. 12. In a different but similar interpretation, H. D. F. Kitto also robs atē of its supernatural element by comparing it to a live wire, something that strikes willy-nilly.

4. For thoughtful and quite different interpretations of the religious dimension of this ode, see C. M. Bowra, Sopho-clean Tragedy (Oxford: Oxford University Press, 1944), Müller's commentary pp. 135-40; Hugh Lloyd-Jones, The Justice of Zeus (Berkeley: University of California Press, 1971), pp. 113-15; and E. R. Dodds, in Greece and Rome 13 (1966): 37-49. Bowra's position has few followers today. Lloyd-Jones rightly points out but exaggerates the emphasis in this play on the curse element. There is, however, no agreement on this or on the general subject of Sophocles' outlook toward his gods (see 450 n.). Dodds (p. 46) summarizes his view of Sophocles' beliefs in two points: 1) Sophocles did not believe, or did not always believe, that the gods are in any human sense "just," and 2) Sophocles always believes that the gods existed and that men should worship them. If Sophocles denies the justice of the gods, he is at variance with the passionate con-viction of believers from Hesiod through Aeschylus to the col-lapse of paganism. Still, Dodds does seem to be right: Sopho-cles is both pious (e.g., believing in the gods' power and personally holding various priesthoods in Athens), and he does not always believe that the gods are in any human sense "just." Sophocles believes in the gods and reveres them despite atē, the divine force that strikes down the heroic Antigone. This strange combination of beliefs is foreign to a Judaeo-Christian milieu. The orthodox Jew or Christian believes in God despite the triumph of evil forces, but he does not make God the ulti-mate source of those evils. Lloyd-Jones tries to avoid Dodds's double conclusion by stressing the natural law in Sophoclean dikē rather than the moral law. He notes (p. 128) that dikē means not only "justice" but also "the order of the universe," and "that order often seems to impose a natural rather than a moral law." What made it hard, he continues, for men to under-stand the justice of the gods "was the immense extent of time which may separate cause from punishment and the complex inter-weaving within human history of different causal chains of injustice followed by chastisement" (p. 128).

5 THE THIRD EPISODE AND THE ODE ON EROS

1. W. J. Ziobro, American Journal of Philology 92 (1971):
81-85. Most critics believe Antigone enters after the Ode on
Eros.
2. Müller (pp. 171 ff.) gives one of the best interpretations of this ode. Some of his points are that the Chorus
mistakenly dismisses Haemon's good advice to his father because
they suppose he is blinded by the power of love; Haemon, in
the episode with Creon, represents the moral right of Antigone,
not his love for her; his love could not be, in his eyes or
hers, a valid argument for her acquittal if she really had
transgressed a legitimate law. See Robert F. Goheen, The
Imagery of Sophocles' Antigone (Princeton: Princeton University
Press, 1951), p. 33, on the imagery of the ode, especially the
metaphor of man, as a horse driven by powers beyond his control (791-92).
3. As early as Homer (Iliad 14. 199-200), Hera asks Aphrodite to "give me love and desire (philotēta kai himeron) with
which you subdue (damnāi) all immortals and mortals alike."
Note the military imagery there as here. The motif is common-
place among the lyric poets and in the choruses of Euripides.
Cf. Euripides' Hippolytos 525 ff. where "Eros brings bewitching grace into the heart of those he would destroy." Later in
the same Euripidean chorus, Eros is the author of dread calam-
ities, bringing ruinous waste upon the world. For the tortured
Phaedra, for her pragmatic nurse, for the proud Aphrodite, and
for the pompous Hippolytos, eros is a disease, a nonmoral state
of mind, even greater than a goddess (359-60), crushing those
who reject its power.
F. Lasserre (La figure d'Eros dans la poésie grecque
[Lausanne, 1946], pp. 66-82) studies Sophocles' ode in the
light of earlier erotic literature and concludes that the
flesh-and-blood god of Anacreon has given way to an Attic god,
"un concept doué d'une forme animée (82)." Although Lasserre
tends to exaggerate the importance of this ode for the whole
play, he does demonstrate not only how different this hymn on
love is from the frivolous, delicate infant god depicted on
the contemporary Parthenon frieze, but also how Sophocles has
endowed eros here with a previously unknown depth.
4. Sophocles' new vision seems to have impressed his
younger contemporary, Euripides. Cf. Medea 844, where eros is
pictured as sitting alongside sophia, wisdom, and collaborating
with her. Denys Page (Euripides' Medea [Oxford: Clarendon,
1938], p. 134, n. 844) observes: the passion commonly limited
to physical love of man and woman is here diverted to other
creatures of beauty--poetry, music, etc.